VIRTUAL HAND SHAKES

The new Frontier of Digital Diplomacy

Table of Contents

Acknowledgment

I would like to express my deepest gratitude to my wife, Addis Moges, whose unwavering support and understanding has been the basis of this endeavor. Your patience, encouragement, and belief in me have sustained me through the highs and lows of the writing process.

Thank you for your sacrifices, for your endless cups of tea during late-night writing sessions, and for your willingness to listen to my ideas, frustrations, and triumphs. Your insight and perspective have enriched this book in ways I could never have imagined.

Forward

As someone deeply immersed in the realms of international relations and diplomacy, my journey into the world of digital diplomacy has been both enlightening and transformative. From my early days as a curious student of Political Science and International Relations at Addis Ababa University to my ongoing pursuit of a PhD in Peace and Security Studies, the evolution of diplomatic practices in the digital age has remained a central theme in my academic and professional pursuits.

During my undergraduate years, the allure of comprehending the complexities of the international system fueled my thirst for knowledge. However, it was my role as a journalist at Addis Media Network, particularly within the English Desk, that provided me with my first insights into the significance of diplomatic affairs. Through crafting news articles on various diplomatic events and issues, I laid the groundwork for my future involvement in digital diplomacy.

My academic journey continued with the attainment of a Master of Arts degree in International Relations and Diplomacy, which further broadened my understanding of global dynamics. It was during this period that I ventured into television journalism, hosting a weekly program called "The Diplomatic Corner." Through this platform, I had the privilege of engaging with numerous ambassadors and scholars, delving into the practical intricacies of diplomacy and international relations.

The onset of the COVID-19 pandemic marked a pivotal moment, thrusting the world of diplomacy into the digital realm. As traditional diplomatic channels transitioned towards virtual summits and digital engagement, I recognized the immense potential of digital technologies in shaping diplomatic discourse and practice.

Amidst Ethiopia's challenges, including the GERD-Nile Politics and the Northern war, I witnessed firsthand the efficacy of digital diplomacy in navigating complex geopolitical landscapes. Stepping onto the digital front, I dedicated myself to campaigns aimed at countering external pressures and advocating for Ethiopia's interests on the global stage.

Through rigorous study and hands-on engagement, I developed a profound appreciation for the role of digital diplomacy in advancing national interests and shaping international discourse. My journey culminates in the creation of this book, "Virtual Handshakes: The new Frontier of Digital Diplomacy," where I aim to illuminate the transformative potential of digital diplomacy for everyone diplomatic pursuits.

Drawing from my accumulated experiences and insights, I endeavor to contribute to the discourse on digital diplomacy, offering a nuanced understanding of its opportunities and challenges. It is my sincere hope that this book serves as a valuable resource for policymakers, diplomats, academics, and students alike, as they navigate the ever-evolving landscape of international relations in the digital age.

Preface

In an era characterized by rapid technological advancements and unprecedented interconnectedness, the landscape of diplomacy is experiencing a profound transformation. The emergence of digital tools and platforms has fundamentally altered how nations interact, communicate, and negotiate on the global stage. As the boundaries between physical and virtual diplomacy blur, understanding this new frontier—Digital Diplomacy—becomes imperative.

"Virtual Handshakes: The New Frontier of Digital Diplomacy" embarks on an illuminating journey into the evolving landscape of international relations in the digital age. From its inception, the book meticulously explores the essence of digital diplomacy, tracing its historical evolution and underscoring its indispensable role in modern diplomatic practices. Through meticulously crafted chapters, readers are guided through the multifaceted dimensions of digital diplomacy, comprehensively exploring its applications, challenges, and future prospects.

The book commences by examining the pivotal role of social media in diplomatic communication, offering real-world case studies and effective engagement strategies. It then delves into virtual public diplomacy, demonstrating how digital platforms bridge cultural divides and foster global understanding. From cyber diplomacy's response to geopolitical challenges to the transformative potential of virtual summits, each chapter provides invaluable insights into this dynamic realm.

Furthermore, "Virtual Handshakes" addresses critical issues such as crisis management, ethical considerations, and the legal dimensions of digital diplomacy. It offers a comprehensive examination of AI governance, data privacy, and transparency in online diplomatic engagement. Additionally, the book pioneers discussions on diplomatic training in the digital age, emphasizing the importance of digital literacy and capacity building for future diplomats.

Moreover, "Virtual Handshakes" explores digital diplomacy's applications across various sectors, including economic diplomacy, environmental cooperation, gender equality, and global health security. With its forward-thinking approach, the book provides readers with a roadmap for navigating the complexities of the future digital landscape.

In the process of writing this book, I have relied on the work of many scholars. I took great care to acknowledge all of them by properly referencing their works in APA style. If unknowingly I left one or more authors unacknowledged, I would like to extend my apologies for such an oversight.

With its blend of scholarly analysis and practical insights, "Virtual Handshakes" stands as an indispensable guide for policymakers, diplomats, scholars, and practitioners, envisioning a future where digital diplomacy shapes a more connected and collaborative world.

PART I

FOUNDATIONS OF DIGITAL DIPLOMACY

1. INTRODUCTION TO DIGITAL DIPLOMACY

"In the age of digital diplomacy, the power of a tweet can sometimes outweigh the impact of a traditional diplomatic cable." – Unknown

In the introductory chapter of "Virtual Handshakes: Exploring the Frontier of Digital Diplomacy," the concept of digital diplomacy is elucidated to provide a foundational understanding of its significance in contemporary international relations. Digital diplomacy, also known as e-diplomacy or cyber diplomacy refers to the use of digital tools and platforms by governments, diplomats, and non-state actors to conduct diplomatic activities, communicate with foreign audiences, and advance national interests in the digital sphere (Fisher, 2017).

One of the key discussions in this chapter revolves around the historical evolution of diplomacy in the digital age. The advent of the internet and the proliferation of digital technologies have revolutionized the practice of diplomacy, fundamentally altering the way states interact and engage with one another on the global stage (Kurbalija, 2019). With the rise of social media, online forums, and virtual summits, traditional diplomatic norms and practices have been reshaped to adapt to the realities of the digital era.

Furthermore, the chapter highlights the importance and relevance of digital diplomacy in contemporary international relations. In an increasingly interconnected world, digital tools have become indispensable instruments for governments to engage with foreign publics, shape narratives, and influence perceptions on a global scale (Seib, 2012). From public diplomacy initiatives on social media to crisis management efforts in cyberspace, digital diplomacy has emerged as a critical component of statecraft in the 21st century.

Moreover, the scope and objectives of the book are delineated to provide readers with a roadmap for navigating the subsequent chapters. By examining the various dimensions of digital diplomacy—from social media engagement to cybersecurity concerns—the book aims to offer a comprehensive overview of this dynamic field and its implications for diplomacy, governance, and international cooperation.

In summary, Chapter 1 serves as a foundational primer on digital diplomacy, setting the stage for deeper exploration into the intricacies of this evolving phenomenon. By elucidating its historical roots, contemporary relevance, and overarching objectives, this chapter lays the groundwork for understanding the transformative impact of digital technologies on the practice of diplomacy in the 21st century.

1.1 Defining digital diplomacy

Digital diplomacy, also known as e-diplomacy or cyber diplomacy encompasses the use of digital technologies and platforms by governments, diplomats, and non-state actors to conduct diplomatic activities, communicate with foreign audiences, and advance national interests in the digital sphere (Fisher, 2017). At its core, digital diplomacy represents an evolution of traditional diplomacy in response to the opportunities and challenges presented by the digital age.

This definition underscores the multifaceted nature of digital diplomacy, which extends beyond the mere use of social media to encompass a wide range of activities and strategies in the digital realm. From virtual summits and online forums to data-driven analysis and cybersecurity initiatives, digital diplomacy encompasses a diverse array of tools and techniques for engaging with foreign counterparts and shaping international relations (Kurbalija, 2019).

Moreover, digital diplomacy is characterized by its dynamic and adaptive nature, reflecting the rapid pace of technological innovation and the evolving dynamics of global politics. As digital technologies continue to evolve, so too do the strategies and tactics employed by diplomats and policymakers to leverage their potential for diplomatic ends (Seib, 2012).

In essence, digital diplomacy represents a paradigm shift in the practice of diplomacy, marking a departure from traditional modes of communication and engagement toward a more decentralized, networked, and participatory approach to international relations. By harnessing the power of digital technologies, diplomats can reach broader audiences, facilitate cross-cultural dialogue, and foster cooperation on shared challenges in ways that were previously unimaginable.

1.2 Historical Evolution of Diplomacy in the Digital Age

The historical evolution of diplomacy in the digital age reflects the profound impact of technological advancements on the practice of international relations. While diplomacy has long been characterized by face-to-face interactions and formalized protocols, the advent of digital technologies has introduced new modes of communication and transformed the dynamics of diplomatic engagement (Gilboa, 2016).

The roots of digital diplomacy can be traced back to the early days of the internet, when governments began to explore the potential of digital platforms for diplomatic communication and information dissemination. In the 1990s, the emergence of email and online forums provided diplomats with new channels for engaging with foreign counterparts and sharing information in real time (Weldes, 2015).

However, it was not until the early 21st century that digital diplomacy began to gain traction as a distinct field of practice. The rise of social media platforms, such as Twitter, Facebook, and YouTube, revolutionized the way governments interacted with foreign audiences and conducted public diplomacy campaigns (Seib, 2012). Diplomats began to use social media to disseminate policy messages, engage with citizens, and shape international perceptions of their countries.

Moreover, the events of the Arab Spring in 2011 highlighted the transformative power of digital technologies in facilitating political mobilization and social change. Governments around the world took note of the role played by social media in these upheavals and began to invest more heavily in digital diplomacy efforts as a means of promoting stability and advancing their strategic interests (Sharp, 2014).

In recent years, the evolution of digital diplomacy has been further accelerated by the proliferation of mobile technologies, big data analytics, and artificial intelligence. These advancements have enabled diplomats to access real-time information, analyze public sentiment, and engage with diverse audiences in more targeted and personalized ways (Zhao, 2019).

Overall, the historical evolution of diplomacy in the digital age underscores the transformative impact of technology on the practice of international relations. From the early days of email communication to the present era of social media engagement and data-driven diplomacy, digital technologies have reshaped the landscape of diplomacy in profound and far-reaching ways.

1.3 Importance and Relevance of Digital Diplomacy in Contemporary International Relations

In contemporary international relations, digital diplomacy has emerged as a critical tool for governments to navigate the complexities of a rapidly changing global landscape. The importance and relevance of digital diplomacy stem from its ability to leverage digital technologies to enhance diplomatic communication, advance national interests, and address transnational challenges in innovative ways (Manor, 2019).

One of the key reasons for the growing importance of digital diplomacy is the increasing interconnectedness of the world in the digital age. With billions of people connected to the internet and active on social media platforms, digital technologies have transformed the way information is disseminated, opinions are formed, and decisions are made on a global scale (Nye, 2019). In this context, digital diplomacy provides governments with unprecedented opportunities to engage with foreign audiences, shape public perceptions, and build relationships beyond traditional diplomatic channels.

Moreover, digital diplomacy plays a crucial role in enhancing diplomatic transparency and accountability in contemporary international relations. Through platforms such as Twitter, Facebook, and Instagram, diplomats can communicate directly with citizens, bypassing traditional media gatekeepers and fostering greater openness and accessibility in diplomatic discourse (Cull, 2019). This increased transparency not only builds trust and credibility but also enables governments to more effectively convey their policy priorities and respond to public concerns in real time.

Furthermore, digital diplomacy is indispensable for addressing transnational challenges that defy traditional borders and require collective action on a global scale. Issues such as climate change, cybersecurity, and pandemic response necessitate cooperation and coordination among nations, which can be facilitated through digital platforms and diplomatic networks (Muller, 2020). By leveraging digital technologies, diplomats can exchange information, share best practices, and mobilize international support for collaborative solutions to shared challenges.

Additionally, digital diplomacy has become increasingly important for projecting soft power and shaping international perceptions of a country's values, culture, and leadership. Through strategic use of social media, cultural exchanges, and public diplomacy campaigns, governments can enhance their global influence, attract investment, and promote tourism (Gilboa, 2018). In an era of information abundance and digital connectivity, the ability to craft compelling narratives and engage audiences across borders is essential for maintaining influence and competitiveness in the international arena.

In summary, the importance and relevance of digital diplomacy in contemporary international relations cannot be overstated. As digital technologies continue to evolve and shape the dynamics of global politics, diplomats must adapt their strategies and embrace new tools to effectively engage with foreign counterparts, address transnational challenges, and advance their countries' interests in the digital age.

1.4 Scope and Objectives of the Book

The scope and objectives of "Virtual Handshakes: Exploring the Frontier of Digital Diplomacy" are delineated to provide readers with a comprehensive understanding of the multifaceted field of digital diplomacy and its implications for contemporary international relations. The book adopts a broad and interdisciplinary approach to digital diplomacy, encompassing diverse topics and perspectives from academia, government, and civil society. It examines the various dimensions of digital diplomacy, including but not limited to:

- The use of social media platforms as diplomatic tools.
- Cyber diplomacy and cybersecurity challenges in the digital age.
- Public diplomacy and cultural exchanges in the virtual realm.
- Crisis management and humanitarian assistance in the digital sphere.
- Legal and ethical considerations of digital diplomacy.
- Diplomatic training and capacity building in the digital era.
- Future trends and emerging technologies in digital diplomacy.

By exploring these topics, the book aims to provide readers with a comprehensive overview of the evolving landscape of digital diplomacy and its implications for diplomacy, governance, and international cooperation. The objectives of the book are fourfold:

1. To provide a nuanced understanding of digital diplomacy as a dynamic and interdisciplinary field of study.
2. To examine the practical applications of digital diplomacy in addressing contemporary diplomatic challenges and opportunities.
3. To assess the impact of digital technologies on traditional diplomatic practices and norms.
4. To offer insights and recommendations for policymakers, diplomats, scholars, and practitioners on how to effectively navigate the complexities of digital diplomacy in the 21st century.

Through a combination of empirical case studies, and practical insights, the book seeks to contribute to scholarly debates on digital diplomacy while also offering practical guidance for diplomatic practitioners and policymakers grappling with the opportunities and challenges of the digital age. Hence, "Virtual Handshakes" aims to serve as a comprehensive and accessible resource for anyone interested in understanding the transformative role of digital technologies in shaping the practice of diplomacy and international relations in the contemporary world.

2. THE ROLE OF SOCIAL MEDIA IN DIPLOMATIC COMMUNICATION

"Social media has transformed diplomacy. Today, a single post has the potential to shape international relations." - Joseph Nye

Social media has indeed revolutionized the practice of diplomacy, providing diplomats and governments with powerful tools to connect with global audiences, communicate policy objectives, and influence international narratives (Manor, 2017). This transformation has fundamentally altered the landscape of diplomatic communication, opening up new channels for engagement and interaction that were previously inaccessible.

Public diplomacy, which involves the strategic communication of a country's values, culture, and policies to foreign audiences, has been profoundly impacted by the rise of social media (Hayden, 2018). Platforms such as Twitter, Facebook, and Instagram allow diplomats to engage directly with citizens around the world, fostering dialogue, promoting cultural exchanges, and shaping perceptions of their countries. Through engaging content, interactive campaigns, and targeted messaging, diplomats can effectively convey their nation's narrative and build positive relationships with global audiences.

Moreover, social media has become an indispensable tool in crisis management for diplomatic missions (Hudson & Thalhammer, 2020). During emergencies such as natural disasters or political unrest, social media platforms enable governments to provide real-time updates, share important information, and coordinate response efforts. By leveraging the immediacy and reach of social media, diplomats can effectively communicate with citizens abroad, offer assistance, and mobilize international support in times of crisis.

Furthermore, social media facilitates direct communication and engagement between diplomats, enhancing bilateral relations and diplomatic cooperation (Jensen, 2017). Platforms like LinkedIn and Twitter allow diplomats to connect with their counterparts, engage in informal dialogue, and establish personal relationships that can pave the way for diplomatic negotiations and collaboration on shared challenges. By fostering mutual understanding and trust, social media strengthens diplomatic ties and promotes peace and cooperation between nations.

In summary, the pivotal role of social media in diplomatic communication cannot be overstated. By offering unprecedented opportunities for engagement, information sharing, and relationship building, social media has transformed diplomacy into a more transparent, dynamic, and inclusive practice. As diplomats and governments continue to adapt to the digital age, social media will remain a central tool for shaping international relations and promoting global cooperation.

2.1 Social Media Platforms as Diplomatic Tools

Social media platforms have emerged as indispensable tools for diplomats and governments, offering unprecedented opportunities to engage with global audiences, convey policy messages, and shape international narratives (Manor, 2017). These platforms serve as dynamic channels for public diplomacy efforts, enabling diplomats to directly interact with citizens, civil society organizations, and foreign publics.

Twitter, Facebook, Instagram, LinkedIn, and YouTube are among the most widely utilized social media platforms in diplomatic communication. Each platform offers unique features and capabilities that diplomats can leverage to effectively reach and engage diverse audiences around the world.

Twitter, with its real-time nature and concise format, has become a preferred platform for diplomats to share updates, express opinions, and engage in public discourse (Hayden, 2018). Diplomats use Twitter to disseminate official statements, respond to inquiries, and participate in online conversations on a wide range of topics, from policy issues to cultural events.

Facebook provides diplomats with a more interactive and visual platform for engaging with audiences through posts, photos, videos, and live streams (Manor, 2017). Diplomatic missions often maintain Facebook pages to share stories, highlight cultural exchanges, and showcase their country's achievements and contributions to the global community.

Instagram has gained popularity among diplomats for its emphasis on visual storytelling and its ability to reach younger audiences (Khan, 2019). Diplomats use Instagram to share behind-the-scenes glimpses of diplomatic life, showcase cultural heritage, and promote tourism and cultural exchanges.

LinkedIn serves as a professional networking platform for diplomats to connect with counterparts, policymakers, and professionals in various fields (Jensen, 2017). Diplomats use LinkedIn to share articles, participate in discussions, and build professional relationships that can contribute to diplomatic cooperation and collaboration.

YouTube offers diplomats a platform to share video content, including speeches, interviews, documentaries, and virtual tours of diplomatic missions (Hayden, 2018). Diplomatic channels on YouTube enable diplomats to reach a global audience and provide engaging multimedia content that enhances understanding of their country's policies and values.

In summary, social media platforms serve as versatile and powerful diplomatic tools, enabling diplomats to engage with diverse audiences, convey their nation's messages, and shape international perceptions. By strategically leveraging these platforms, diplomats can enhance transparency, foster dialogue, and promote mutual understanding in the digital age.

2.2 Case Studies: Successful Utilization of Social Media in Diplomacy

In examining the successful utilization of social media in diplomacy, several case studies offer valuable insights into how digital platforms have been effectively leveraged by governments and diplomats to achieve diplomatic objectives. These case studies highlight innovative approaches, best practices, and lessons learned from real-world examples of social media diplomacy.

United States Department of State's Twitter Diplomacy: The United States Department of State has been at the forefront of using Twitter as a diplomatic tool, particularly during crises and conflicts. One notable example is the use of Twitter during the Arab Spring uprisings in 2011, where the State Department utilized the platform to communicate with local populations, provide updates on US policy positions, and counter disinformation. By engaging directly with citizens and amplifying messages of support for democratic movements, the US demonstrated the power of social media in shaping perceptions and influencing outcomes in international crises (Sharp, 2014).

Sweden's Digital Diplomacy Campaigns: The Swedish Foreign Ministry has been praised for its innovative and engaging digital diplomacy campaigns on social media platforms. Through initiatives such as the "Sweden on Air" project, which invited citizens to curate and share their experiences of Sweden through social media, Sweden effectively showcased its cultural heritage, values, and policies to a global audience.

By harnessing user-generated content and leveraging the viral nature of social media, Sweden successfully promoted its brand and enhanced its soft power on the international stage (Oklobdzija, 2019).

India's Vaccine Diplomacy on Twitter: During the COVID-19 pandemic, India utilized social media, particularly Twitter, as a diplomatic tool to showcase its vaccine diplomacy efforts. Through the hashtag #VaccineMaitri (Vaccine Friendship), India highlighted its role as a global provider of COVID-19 vaccines, sharing updates on vaccine donations to other countries and showcasing solidarity with the international community. By leveraging social media to amplify its humanitarian efforts and diplomatic outreach, India enhanced its global reputation as a responsible global actor and strengthened diplomatic ties with recipient countries (Singh, 2021).

South Africa's Digital Diplomacy during the Nelson Mandela Funeral: During the funeral of Nelson Mandela in 2013, South Africa effectively utilized social media platforms to engage with global audiences and convey messages of unity and reconciliation. The South African government's official Twitter account, @GovernmentZA, provided real-time updates on the funeral proceedings, shared quotes from Mandela's speeches, and conveyed messages of gratitude to world leaders and citizens for their support. Through its digital diplomacy efforts, South Africa showcased Mandela's legacy and promoted the country as a beacon of democracy and human rights in Africa (Potgieter, 2015).

Ethiopia's Social Media Engagement in Conflict Resolution: While Ethiopia has faced internal conflicts and regional tensions, there are instances where social media has played a role in diplomatic efforts to resolve disputes. For example, during the diplomatic negotiations between Ethiopia and Eritrea in 2018, social media platforms such as Twitter served as channels for official statements, announcements, and updates on the peace process. Ethiopian diplomats utilized Twitter to engage with Eritrean counterparts, share messages of goodwill, and convey the progress of negotiations to the international community. This digital diplomacy approach helped build momentum for peace and contributed to the historic peace agreement between Ethiopia and Eritrea (Tesfaye, 2019).

These case studies illustrate the diverse ways in which social media platforms can be effectively utilized in diplomacy, from crisis communication and public engagement to cultural diplomacy and humanitarian outreach. By examining successful examples of social media diplomacy, diplomats and policymakers can gain valuable insights and inspiration for their own digital diplomacy initiatives.

2.3 Challenges and Risks of Social Media Diplomacy

While social media offers diplomats and governments unprecedented opportunities for engagement and communication, it also presents a range of challenges and risks that must be navigated carefully. Some of the key challenges and risks associated with social media diplomacy:

Misinformation and Disinformation: Social media platforms are rife with misinformation and disinformation, which can spread rapidly and undermine diplomatic efforts (Wang, 2020). False narratives, conspiracy theories, and fake news can erode trust, fuel conflict, and distort public perceptions, posing significant challenges for diplomats seeking to convey accurate information and shape international narratives.

Diplomatic Gaffes and Miscommunication: The fast-paced and informal nature of social media can increase the risk of diplomatic gaffes and miscommunication (Khan, 2019). Diplomats may inadvertently post inappropriate or insensitive content, make factual errors, or engage in online disputes that damage diplomatic relations and undermine credibility. Such incidents can have serious consequences for diplomatic reputation and effectiveness.

Cybersecurity Threats: Social media platforms are vulnerable to cybersecurity threats, including hacking, phishing, and data breaches (Sharikov & Guseva, 2019). Diplomatic missions may be targeted by malicious actors seeking to steal sensitive information, disrupt operations, or manipulate online content for political purposes. Protecting diplomatic communications and ensuring the security of digital infrastructure are critical priorities for diplomats in the age of social media.

Amplification of Diplomatic Tensions: Social media can amplify diplomatic tensions and exacerbate conflicts by providing a platform for inflammatory rhetoric and hostile interactions (Khan, 2019). Diplomatic disputes and crises may escalate quickly on social media, leading to public spats, online campaigns, and diplomatic fallout that complicates efforts to resolve conflicts through traditional diplomatic channels.

Ethical Dilemmas: Social media raises ethical dilemmas for diplomats, who must navigate issues such as privacy, transparency, and freedom of expression (Sharikov & Guseva, 2019). Diplomats must balance the need for openness and engagement with the need to protect sensitive information and uphold diplomatic protocol. Striking the right balance between transparency and discretion is essential for maintaining trust and credibility in diplomatic communication.

Social media diplomacy presents diplomats and governments with a complex array of challenges and risks that require careful consideration and strategic management. By proactively addressing these challenges and adopting robust risk mitigation strategies, diplomats can harness the potential of social media to enhance diplomatic engagement, promote dialogue, and advance national interests in the digital age.

2.4 Strategies for Effective Social Media Engagement in Diplomacy

To navigate the complexities of social media diplomacy and maximize its impact, diplomats and governments can employ a range of strategies aimed at enhancing engagement, promoting transparency, and building credibility. Some of strategies for effective social media engagement in diplomacy are:

Develop a Clear Strategy: Before engaging on social media, diplomats should develop a clear strategy outlining their objectives, target audiences, key messages, and metrics for success (Hudson & Thalhammer, 2020). A well-defined strategy will guide diplomatic efforts, ensure consistency in messaging, and enable diplomats to measure the effectiveness of their social media activities.

Establish an Authentic Voice: Authenticity is crucial in social media diplomacy, as audiences expect genuine, human interactions rather than scripted corporate messaging (Manor, 2017). Diplomats should strive to communicate in a conversational tone, share personal insights and experiences, and engage with followers in a transparent and authentic manner.

Listen and Respond: Social media is a two-way communication channel, and diplomats should actively listen to feedback, monitor conversations, and respond to inquiries from followers (Jensen, 2017). By engaging in dialogue and addressing concerns raised by their audience, diplomats can build trust, foster goodwill, and demonstrate responsiveness to ***public concerns.***

Tell Compelling Stories: Storytelling is a powerful tool in social media diplomacy, allowing diplomats to humanize their messages and connect with audiences on an emotional level (Hayden, 2018). Diplomats should use storytelling techniques to share narratives that illustrate their country's values, achievements, and contributions to the global community.

Cultivate Relationships: Building relationships is essential in social media diplomacy, and diplomats should actively engage with influencers, journalists, and other stakeholders in their online networks (Khan, 2019). By collaborating with influential voices and forging partnerships with key stakeholders, diplomats can amplify their messages and extend their reach to new audiences.

Use Multimedia Content: Visual and multimedia content such as photos, videos, and infographics are highly engaging on social media and can help diplomats convey complex ideas and messages in a compelling and accessible format (Hudson & Thalhammer, 2020). Diplomats should leverage multimedia content to enhance the visibility and impact of their social media efforts.

Monitor and Evaluate: Continuous monitoring and evaluation are essential to gauge the effectiveness of social media engagement and identify areas for improvement (Sharikov & Guseva, 2019). Diplomats should track key metrics such as engagement rates, reach, and sentiment analysis to assess the impact of their social media activities and refine their strategies accordingly.

By adopting these strategies, diplomats and governments can harness the potential of social media to enhance diplomatic engagement, promote dialogue, and advance national interests in the digital age.

3. VIRTUAL PUBLIC DIPLOMACY: BUILDING BRIDGES BETWEEN CULTURES

"Digital diplomacy is not just about connecting governments; it's about connecting people and fostering understanding between cultures." - Alec Ross

Virtual public diplomacy embodies a revolutionary shift in the way nations interact and engage with one another on the global stage. It capitalizes on the vast array of digital technologies available today to transcend geographical barriers and facilitate meaningful connections between people from different cultures, backgrounds, and nations. This chapter embarks on a journey to delve deeper into the essence of virtual public diplomacy, uncovering its profound implications for international relations in the digital age.

At its core, virtual public diplomacy serves as a catalyst for cross-cultural dialogue and exchange, fostering an environment where individuals can engage in open and constructive conversations regardless of physical distance. Through various digital platforms such as social media, online forums, and virtual events, people from diverse cultural backgrounds can come together to share perspectives, exchange ideas, and explore common interests. By facilitating these interactions, virtual public diplomacy promotes mutual understanding, empathy, and respect among nations, laying the foundation for stronger diplomatic relations and cooperation.

Moreover, virtual public diplomacy plays a pivotal role in shaping perceptions and narratives about countries and their people. Through strategic storytelling, cultural showcases, and digital campaigns, nations can convey a nuanced and authentic portrayal of their values, traditions, and contributions to the global community. By highlighting cultural heritage, promoting artistic expressions, and showcasing innovations, virtual public diplomacy enables nations to cultivate positive perceptions and counter misconceptions or stereotypes that may exist in the international arena.

Furthermore, virtual public diplomacy acts as a bridge-builder between nations, forging connections and collaborations that transcend political differences and geopolitical tensions. By providing a platform for cultural exchanges, educational programs, and collaborative projects, virtual diplomacy strengthens people-to-people ties and fosters a sense of global citizenship and solidarity. These connections not only enhance bilateral relations but also contribute to broader efforts towards peace, stability, and prosperity in the interconnected world of the 21st century.

In essence, this chapter explores the transformative potential of virtual public diplomacy as a force for positive change in international relations. By harnessing the power of digital technologies to foster dialogue, promote understanding, and cultivate relationships, virtual public diplomacy offers a pathway towards a more inclusive, interconnected, and harmonious world.

3.1 Concept and Significance of Public Diplomacy in the Digital Era

Public diplomacy, traditionally defined as the communication and engagement efforts undertaken by governments to influence foreign public opinion and promote their national interests, has undergone significant transformation in the digital era (Cull, 2019). This section explores the concept and significance of public diplomacy in the context of the digital age, highlighting its evolving role and impact on international relations.

In the digital era, public diplomacy encompasses a wide range of activities conducted through digital channels such as social media, websites, blogs, podcasts, and online forums (Hayden, 2018). These digital platforms offer diplomats and governments unprecedented opportunities to engage directly with global audiences, share information, and shape perceptions in real-time.

The significance of public diplomacy in the digital era lies in its ability to bridge cultural divides, foster dialogue, and build relationships between nations (Manor, 2017). Digital technologies enable diplomats to engage with foreign publics in ways that were previously unimaginable, facilitating cross-cultural exchanges, promoting mutual understanding, and laying the groundwork for cooperation on shared challenges.

Moreover, public diplomacy in the digital era plays a critical role in advancing national interests and soft power objectives on the global stage (Cull, 2019). By effectively communicating their country's values, policies, and achievements, diplomats can enhance their nation's reputation, influence international perceptions, and shape the broader narrative surrounding key issues in international affairs.

Furthermore, public diplomacy in the digital era is characterized by its interactive and participatory nature, allowing for greater engagement and collaboration between governments, civil society organizations, and foreign audiences (Jensen, 2017). Social media platforms, in particular, enable diplomats to engage in direct dialogue with citizens, respond to inquiries, and address concerns raised by their audience, fostering transparency and accountability in diplomatic communication.

In summary, public diplomacy remains a crucial instrument of statecraft in the digital era, offering diplomats and governments powerful tools to engage with global audiences, convey their nation's messages, and advance their strategic interests on the world stage. By leveraging digital technologies and embracing innovative approaches to communication, diplomats can enhance the effectiveness and impact of public diplomacy efforts in an increasingly interconnected and digitalized world.

3.2 Leveraging Cultural Diplomacy through Virtual Platforms

Cultural diplomacy, the use of cultural exchange and engagement as a means of fostering understanding and cooperation between nations, has found new avenues for expression and impact through virtual platforms in the digital era (Riordan, 2020). This section explores the concept of leveraging cultural diplomacy through virtual platforms, highlighting its significance and potential for promoting cross-cultural dialogue and mutual understanding.

Virtual platforms offer diplomats and cultural actors unprecedented opportunities to showcase their nation's cultural heritage, traditions, and values to global audiences (Falk, 2017). Through virtual exhibitions, online performances, digital archives, and interactive experiences, cultural diplomats can reach diverse audiences around the world and promote cultural exchange in ways that transcend geographic boundaries.

The significance of leveraging cultural diplomacy through virtual platforms lies in its ability to promote cross-cultural dialogue, foster empathy, and build bridges between nations (Hoffmann, 2018). Virtual cultural exchanges enable individuals from different backgrounds to connect, share experiences, and engage in meaningful interactions that promote mutual understanding and appreciation of cultural diversity.

Moreover, virtual platforms offer a cost-effective and accessible means of cultural diplomacy, democratizing access to cultural resources and eliminating barriers to participation (Stelma, 2021). Virtual exhibitions and performances can reach audiences in remote or underserved regions, enabling greater inclusivity and participation in cultural exchange activities.

Furthermore, leveraging cultural diplomacy through virtual platforms enables diplomats to adapt to the challenges posed by the COVID-19 pandemic and other disruptions to traditional diplomatic activities (Riordan, 2020). Virtual cultural events and initiatives provide diplomats with alternative channels for engagement, allowing them to continue promoting cultural exchange and cooperation even in times of crisis.

In summary, leveraging cultural diplomacy through virtual platforms represents a valuable and innovative approach to promoting cross-cultural understanding and cooperation in the digital era. By harnessing the power of virtual technology, diplomats and cultural actors can reach global audiences, foster dialogue, and build relationships that transcend borders, contributing to a more interconnected and harmonious world.

3.3 Virtual Cultural Exchanges and Collaborations

Virtual cultural exchanges and collaborations represent innovative approaches to cultural diplomacy, enabling diplomats, artists, cultural institutions, and audiences to engage in cross-cultural dialogue and cooperation without the need for physical travel or in-person events (Hoffmann, 2018). This section explores the concept of virtual cultural exchanges and collaborations, highlighting their significance and potential for promoting cultural understanding and collaboration on a global scale.

Virtual cultural exchanges involve the sharing of cultural resources, experiences, and perspectives through digital platforms such as online exhibitions, virtual tours, live-streamed performances, and interactive workshops (Falk, 2017). These exchanges enable individuals from different countries and backgrounds to connect, learn from one another, and engage in meaningful cultural interactions that foster mutual understanding and appreciation.

Collaborations between cultural institutions and artists from different countries further enhance the impact and reach of virtual cultural exchanges (Stelma, 2021). By leveraging digital technology, artists can collaborate remotely on joint projects, performances, and exhibitions that transcend geographic boundaries and showcase the richness and diversity of global culture.

The significance of virtual cultural exchanges and collaborations lies in their ability to promote cultural diversity, inclusivity, and dialogue in an increasingly interconnected world (Hoffmann, 2018). By facilitating encounters between individuals from diverse backgrounds and fostering empathy and understanding, virtual cultural exchanges contribute to the promotion of peace, tolerance, and intercultural harmony.

Moreover, virtual cultural exchanges and collaborations offer opportunities for cultural diplomacy that are accessible, cost-effective, and sustainable (Riordan, 2020). By eliminating barriers to participation such as travel costs and logistical challenges, virtual platforms democratize access to cultural resources and enable greater participation in cultural exchange activities.

In summary, virtual cultural exchanges and collaborations represent powerful tools for promoting cultural understanding, cooperation, and dialogue in the digital age. By harnessing the potential of digital technology, diplomats, artists, and cultural institutions can transcend geographic boundaries, connect with global audiences, and build relationships that contribute to a more peaceful, inclusive, and interconnected world.

3.4 Evaluating the Impact of Virtual Public Diplomacy Initiatives

Evaluating the impact of virtual public diplomacy initiatives is essential for diplomats and policymakers to assess the effectiveness of their efforts, identify areas for improvement, and demonstrate the value of cultural exchange and engagement in achieving diplomatic objectives (Melissen, 2017). To explore strategies for evaluating the impact of virtual public diplomacy initiatives, the following highlights are key considerations and methodologies.

Define Clear Objectives: Before evaluating the impact of virtual public diplomacy initiatives, diplomats should define clear and measurable objectives that align with their broader diplomatic goals (Snow & Taylor, 2020). Whether the objective is to increase cultural understanding, promote dialogue, or enhance bilateral relations, having clearly defined goals will facilitate more meaningful evaluation.

Identify Key Performance Indicators (KPIs): Once objectives are established, diplomats should identify key performance indicators (KPIs) to measure the success of their virtual public diplomacy initiatives (Melissen, 2017). KPIs may include metrics such as audience reach, engagement rates, website traffic, social media interactions and qualitative feedback from participants.

Utilize Data Analytics: Data analytics tools can provide valuable insights into the impact and effectiveness of virtual public diplomacy initiatives (Snow & Taylor, 2020). By analyzing data on website traffic, social media engagement, and audience demographics, diplomats can track trends, identify patterns, and measure the impact of their digital outreach efforts.

Conduct Surveys and Feedback Mechanisms: Surveys and feedback mechanisms can provide valuable qualitative insights into the impact of virtual public diplomacy initiatives (Melissen, 2017). Diplomats can solicit feedback from participants through online surveys, interviews, focus groups, and comment sections to gauge their perceptions, attitudes, and experiences.

Monitor Media Coverage: Monitoring media coverage and public discourse surrounding virtual public diplomacy initiatives can offer insights into their impact on shaping international perceptions and narratives (Snow & Taylor, 2020). Media monitoring tools can track mentions, sentiment, and themes related to diplomatic initiatives in traditional and digital media.

Engage in Stakeholder Consultations: Engaging with stakeholders, including participants, partners, and host countries, can provide valuable perspectives on the impact of virtual public diplomacy initiatives (Melissen, 2017). Diplomats can conduct consultations and debriefings with stakeholders to gather feedback, assess outcomes, and identify lessons learned.

Continuously Evaluate and Adapt: Evaluation of virtual public diplomacy initiatives should be an ongoing and iterative process, with diplomats continuously monitoring and adapting their strategies based on feedback and performance data (Snow & Taylor, 2020). By evaluating outcomes in real-time and making adjustments as needed, diplomats can maximize the impact and effectiveness of their digital engagement efforts.

Evaluating the impact of virtual public diplomacy initiatives is essential for diplomats to assess the effectiveness of their digital outreach efforts, demonstrate value to stakeholders, and inform future strategic planning. By defining clear objectives, identifying key performance indicators, utilizing data analytics, soliciting feedback, monitoring media coverage, engaging stakeholders, and continuously evaluating and adapting strategies, diplomats can ensure that their virtual public diplomacy initiatives contribute to the achievement of broader diplomatic goals in the digital age.

4. CYBER DIPLOMACY: NAVIGATING THE GEOPOLITICAL TERRAIN

"In the age of cyber diplomacy, the battlefield is virtual, but the consequences are very real." – Anonymous

Cyber diplomacy has emerged as a critical dimension of modern diplomacy, shaping international relations and influencing geopolitical dynamics in the digital age. In today's interconnected world, where cyberspace serves as a crucial domain for communication, commerce, and conflict, diplomacy plays a pivotal role in managing the opportunities and challenges posed by the digital revolution.

One of the primary roles of cyber diplomacy is to address global challenges related to cybersecurity. With the proliferation of cyber threats, including cybercrime, espionage, and sabotage, diplomats are increasingly tasked with developing cooperative strategies to enhance cyber resilience and protect critical infrastructure (Klimburg, 2018). Through diplomatic channels, nations can share information, coordinate responses, and establish norms and rules to promote stability and security in cyberspace.

Moreover, cyber diplomacy plays a crucial role in managing cyber threats that transcend national borders. In an era where cyber attacks can have far-reaching consequences and destabilize entire regions, diplomatic efforts are essential for mitigating conflicts, de-escalating tensions, and fostering trust and cooperation among nations (Schmitt, 2017). By engaging in diplomatic dialogue and negotiation, states can work towards consensus on cybersecurity issues and build the foundations for a more secure and resilient digital environment.

Furthermore, cyber diplomacy is instrumental in navigating the complex geopolitics of cyberspace. As digital technologies increasingly intersect with traditional notions of national security and sovereignty, diplomats must navigate a complex web of interests, alliances, and rivalries in the digital domain (Libicki, 2017). From state-sponsored cyber attacks to digital espionage and information warfare, the geopolitical implications of cyber activities are profound, shaping the strategic calculus of nations and influencing global power dynamics.

Cyber diplomacy plays a multifaceted role in addressing global challenges, managing cyber threats, and navigating the complex geopolitics of cyberspace. By leveraging diplomatic channels and strategies, nations can promote stability, security, and cooperation in the digital age, ensuring that the benefits of the digital revolution are maximized while mitigating the risks and challenges posed by cyber threats.

4.1 Understanding Cyber Diplomacy and Its Components

Cyber diplomacy encompasses a broad spectrum of diplomatic efforts aimed at addressing issues related to cyberspace, including cybersecurity, internet governance, and digital rights. This section delves into the various components of cyber diplomacy, providing a comprehensive overview of its key elements. (1), Cybersecurity Cooperation; one of the central components of cyber diplomacy is cybersecurity cooperation, which involves collaborative efforts between nations to enhance cyber resilience, combat cyber threats, and protect critical infrastructure (Dunn Cavelty & Suter, 2019). This includes initiatives such as information sharing, capacity-building programs, and joint exercises aimed at improving cybersecurity capabilities and promoting collective defense against cyber attacks. (2), Norms and Rules; Cyber diplomacy also involves the development and promotion of norms and rules for responsible behavior in cyberspace (Schmitt, 2017).

Diplomatic efforts seek to establish consensus on principles such as the protection of civilian infrastructure, the prohibition of cyber attacks against critical services, and the respect for international law in cyberspace. By fostering adherence to these norms, diplomats aim to reduce the risk of conflict and promote stability in cyberspace. (3), Internet Governance;Internet governance is another key aspect of cyber diplomacy, involving discussions and negotiations on the management and regulation of the internet (DeNardis, 2020). Diplomats engage in forums such as the Internet Governance Forum (IGF) and the International Telecommunication Union (ITU) to address issues such as domain name management, data privacy, and digital rights. By promoting an inclusive and multistakeholder approach to internet governance, diplomats aim to ensure the openness, interoperability, and security of the global internet infrastructure. (4), Digital Rights and Freedoms; Cyber diplomacy also encompasses efforts to promote and protect digital rights and freedoms, including freedom of expression, privacy, and access to information (MacKinnon, 2012). Diplomatic initiatives seek to address challenges such as censorship, surveillance, and online censorship, advocating for policies and practices that uphold human rights principles in the digital realm. By engaging in diplomatic dialogue and advocacy, diplomats aim to ensure that the benefits of the internet are enjoyed by all, while mitigating the risks of abuse and exploitation.

Cyber diplomacy encompasses a range of components aimed at addressing challenges and opportunities in cyberspace. From cybersecurity cooperation and the development of norms and rules to internet governance and the protection of digital rights, diplomats play a crucial role in shaping the future of the digital domain through diplomatic engagement and negotiation.

4.2 Addressing Cybersecurity Challenges in Diplomatic Relations

Cybersecurity challenges pose significant threats to diplomatic relations between nations, requiring careful diplomatic engagement and cooperation to mitigate risks and foster trust. This section explores the key cybersecurity challenges faced in diplomatic relations and examines diplomatic strategies for addressing these challenges effectively. (1), Cyber Espionage and Intelligence Gathering; One of the primary cybersecurity challenges in diplomatic relations is cyber espionage, where nations conduct covert operations to gather intelligence and sensitive information from foreign governments (Rid, 2019).

Diplomats must navigate the delicate balance between intelligence gathering and diplomatic engagement, ensuring that cybersecurity concerns do not undermine trust and cooperation between nations. Transparency, dialogue, and confidence-building measures are essential for addressing concerns related to cyber espionage and safeguarding diplomatic relations. (2), State-Sponsored Cyber Attacks; State-sponsored cyber attacks pose another significant challenge to diplomatic relations, with nations targeting each other's critical infrastructure, government networks, and private sector entities for political or strategic purposes (Lindsay, 2019).

Diplomatic responses to state-sponsored cyber attacks often involve diplomatic protests, sanctions, or retaliatory measures, aimed at holding perpetrators accountable and deterring future cyber aggression. Establishing clear norms and rules for responsible behavior in cyberspace is essential for reducing the risk of conflict and promoting stability in diplomatic relations. (3), Cyber Threats to Diplomatic Communications; Protecting diplomatic communications from cyber threats is a critical priority for diplomats, given the sensitive nature of diplomatic exchanges and negotiations (Lewis, 2018).

Diplomatic missions must implement robust cybersecurity measures to safeguard classified information, sensitive communications, and diplomatic channels from unauthorized access or interception. Encryption, secure communication protocols, and cybersecurity training for diplomatic staff are essential for mitigating the risk of cyber threats to diplomatic communications. (4), Cyber Diplomacy and Confidence-Building Measures; Diplomatic engagement plays a crucial role in addressing cybersecurity challenges and building trust between nations (Schmitt, 2017).

Cyber diplomacy initiatives, such as bilateral cybersecurity dialogues, confidence-building measures, and joint cybersecurity exercises, provide platforms for dialogue, cooperation, and collaboration on cybersecurity issues. By promoting transparency, information sharing, and mutual understanding, diplomats can enhance cybersecurity resilience and strengthen diplomatic relations in the face of cyber threats.

In conclusion, addressing cybersecurity challenges in diplomatic relations requires proactive engagement, cooperation, and diplomacy. By acknowledging the shared interests and mutual vulnerabilities in cyberspace, diplomats can work together to develop effective strategies for mitigating cyber threats, promoting cybersecurity resilience, and safeguarding diplomatic relations in the digital age.

4.3 International Cyber Norms and Diplomatic Cooperation

International cyber norms play a crucial role in shaping diplomatic cooperation and promoting stability in cyberspace. This section explores the significance of international cyber norms and examines the role of diplomatic cooperation in their development and implementation.

International cyber norms are principles of responsible behavior in cyberspace that guide the conduct of states and promote stability, security, and cooperation (Tikk & Russell, 2020). These norms include principles such as the prohibition of cyber attacks against critical infrastructure, the protection of civilian networks, and the respect for international law in cyberspace. Diplomatic efforts are essential for establishing consensus on cyber norms and encouraging adherence to these principles by nations.

Diplomatic cooperation plays a crucial role in the development and promotion of international cyber norms (Schmitt, 2017). Through multilateral forums, such as the United Nations, the Organization for Security and Cooperation in Europe (OSCE), and the Group of Governmental Experts (GGE) on cybersecurity, diplomats engage in negotiations, dialogue, and consensus-building to develop common understandings and agreements on cyber norms. By fostering dialogue and cooperation, diplomats can bridge differences, build trust, and promote consensus on cyber norms among nations with diverse interests and perspectives.

Once established, international cyber norms require diplomatic engagement and implementation to ensure compliance and effectiveness (Stanger, 2019). Diplomats play a key role in promoting adherence to cyber norms through diplomatic engagement, persuasion, and enforcement mechanisms. This includes diplomatic protests, sanctions, and diplomatic demarches in response to violations of cyber norms, as well as diplomatic initiatives to promote awareness, capacity-building, and confidence-building measures among nations.

Diplomatic cooperation is also essential for monitoring and verifying compliance with international cyber norms (Nye, 2021). Through diplomatic channels, nations exchange information, share best practices, and collaborate on monitoring mechanisms to assess compliance with cyber norms and identify instances of non-compliance or suspicious activities. By promoting transparency and accountability, diplomats can strengthen the credibility and effectiveness of international cyber norms and foster trust and confidence among nations.

In summary, international cyber norms and diplomatic cooperation are essential for promoting stability, security, and cooperation in cyberspace. Through diplomatic engagement, negotiation, and implementation, diplomats play a critical role in developing, promoting, and enforcing cyber norms, thereby contributing to a safer and more secure digital environment for all.

4.4 The Role of Cyber Diplomacy in Conflict Resolution and Prevention

Cyber diplomacy plays a critical role in conflict resolution and prevention in the digital age, offering diplomatic avenues to address cyber conflicts, mitigate tensions, and promote stability in cyberspace. This section examines the multifaceted role of cyber diplomacy in conflict resolution and prevention, highlighting its importance in managing cyber conflicts and preventing escalation into broader geopolitical crises.

Cyber diplomacy serves as a vital tool for preventing the escalation of cyber conflicts into full-blown international crises (Nakashima & Nakashima, 2019). Diplomatic efforts focus on de-escalating tensions, fostering dialogue, and promoting restraint among nations engaged in cyber disputes. By engaging in diplomatic dialogue and negotiation, diplomats seek to address grievances, clarify intentions, and find peaceful solutions to cyber conflicts before they escalate into broader conflicts.

Confidence-building measures (CBMs) are another key aspect of cyber diplomacy aimed at reducing mistrust and promoting transparency among nations (Stanger, 2019). Diplomatic initiatives such as bilateral cybersecurity dialogues, joint cyber exercises, and information-sharing mechanisms help build trust, enhance communication, and reduce the risk of misunderstandings and miscalculations in cyberspace. By promoting confidence and predictability, diplomats can help prevent conflicts and minimize the potential for misperceptions and unintended escalation.

In the event of a cyber crisis or incident, cyber diplomacy plays a crucial role in facilitating crisis management and conflict resolution efforts (Libicki, 2017). Diplomats serve as mediators, facilitators, and negotiators, helping parties involved in a cyber conflict to communicate, de-escalate tensions, and find mutually acceptable solutions. Through diplomatic channels, diplomats can engage in shuttle diplomacy, backchannel negotiations, and crisis communication to defuse crises and prevent further escalation.

Cyber diplomacy also contributes to conflict prevention by strengthening international norms and rules for responsible behavior in cyberspace (Schmitt, 2017). Diplomatic efforts focus on promoting adherence to established norms such as the protection of civilian infrastructure, the prohibition of cyber attacks against critical services, and the respect for international law in cyberspace. By reinforcing these norms through diplomatic engagement and enforcement mechanisms, diplomats help create a more stable and predictable cyber environment, reducing the likelihood of conflicts and promoting responsible state behavior.

In summary, cyber diplomacy plays a crucial role in conflict resolution and prevention by preventing escalation, promoting confidence-building measures, facilitating crisis management, and strengthening international norms and rules in cyberspace. By leveraging diplomatic channels and strategies, diplomats can help manage cyber conflicts, mitigate tensions, and promote stability and security in the digital age.

5. Virtual Summits and Conferences: Redefining Diplomatic Gatherings

"In the digital age, diplomacy is not just conducted in conference rooms but also in chat rooms, forums, and encrypted channels." – Anonymous

Virtual summits and conferences have emerged as transformative tools in modern diplomacy, reshaping the way diplomats engage, negotiate, and collaborate on global issues. The evolution of digital technology and the global COVID-19 pandemic have accelerated the adoption of virtual platforms, making virtual gatherings a crucial component of diplomatic practice. This chapter explores the multifaceted nature of virtual summits and conferences, examining their benefits, challenges, and implications for diplomatic relations and outcomes.

Virtual diplomatic gatherings offer numerous advantages over traditional in-person events, including increased accessibility, cost-effectiveness, and flexibility. With virtual platforms, diplomats can participate in meetings and conferences from anywhere in the world, eliminating the need for extensive travel and reducing associated costs. Additionally, virtual gatherings accommodate diverse schedules and time zones, making it easier for diplomats from different regions to engage in diplomatic discussions and negotiations (Choudhury et al., 2020). This accessibility enhances the inclusivity of diplomatic processes, allowing for broader participation and representation from a diverse range of stakeholders.

Despite their benefits, virtual summits and conferences also present challenges and limitations that must be addressed. Technical issues such as internet connectivity and platform reliability can disrupt proceedings and hinder effective communication among participants. Moreover, virtual platforms may lack the interpersonal dynamics and networking opportunities associated with face-to-face interactions, potentially limiting the depth of engagement and relationship-building among diplomats (Lopez-Tarruella, 2021). Overcoming these challenges requires innovative solutions and strategies to ensure the seamless operation and effectiveness of virtual diplomatic gatherings.

The shift towards virtual diplomacy has significant implications for diplomatic practices and outcomes. Virtual platforms influence negotiation dynamics, decision-making processes, and the conduct of diplomacy in profound ways. Diplomats must adapt to new tools and techniques for engaging in virtual diplomacy, from virtual breakout sessions to digital document sharing and collaborative tools (Kotliar et al., 2021). Additionally, virtual gatherings facilitate innovative approaches to diplomatic engagement, such as virtual reality simulations and augmented reality experiences, which enhance collaboration and problem-solving among participants.

Looking ahead, the future of virtual summits and conferences holds promise for further innovation and evolution in diplomatic practice. As technology continues to advance, diplomats must remain agile and adaptable in harnessing the potential of virtual platforms for diplomatic engagement. Policymakers must also address issues related to digital inclusivity, cybersecurity, and data privacy to ensure that virtual gatherings remain accessible, secure, and transparent (Fischer et al., 2022). By embracing virtual diplomacy and leveraging digital tools strategically, diplomats can enhance diplomatic outcomes, promote international cooperation, and address global challenges in the 21st century.

5.1 Evolution of Virtual Summits and Conferences

The evolution of virtual summits and conferences represents a significant paradigm shift in diplomatic engagement, driven by advancements in digital technology and the changing dynamics of global diplomacy. Initially, virtual gatherings were primarily seen as alternatives to in-person events, offering convenience and cost-effectiveness for participants. However, their evolution has been accelerated by factors such as the global COVID-19 pandemic, which necessitated the adoption of virtual platforms for diplomatic engagement (Choudhury et al., 2020).

The early stages of virtual summits and conferences were characterized by experimentation and adaptation, as diplomats and organizers sought to replicate the dynamics of traditional in-person gatherings in the digital realm. Basic video conferencing tools were used to facilitate discussions and negotiations, albeit with limitations in terms of interactivity and functionality. Over time, technological advancements and the development of specialized virtual event platforms have transformed virtual gatherings into sophisticated and immersive experiences (Fischer et al., 2022).

The global COVID-19 pandemic served as a catalyst for the widespread adoption of virtual summits and conferences, as travel restrictions and health concerns made in-person events impractical or impossible. Diplomatic institutions and organizations quickly pivoted to virtual platforms to ensure continuity in diplomatic engagement and decision-making processes. As a result, virtual summits and conferences have become integral components of diplomatic practice, offering diplomats new opportunities for engagement and collaboration in the digital age (Kotliar et al., 2021).

Looking ahead, the evolution of virtual summits and conferences is expected to continue, driven by ongoing technological innovation and shifts in diplomatic practice. Virtual reality (VR) and augmented reality (AR) technologies hold promise for creating more immersive and interactive virtual experiences, allowing participants to engage in diplomatic discussions and negotiations in virtual environments that simulate real-world interactions. Additionally, advances in artificial intelligence (AI) and natural language processing (NLP) are enabling new capabilities such as real-time translation and transcription, further enhancing the accessibility and inclusivity of virtual gatherings (Lopez-Tarruella, 2021).

In summary, the evolution of virtual summits and conferences represents a transformative shift in diplomatic engagement, offering diplomats new opportunities for collaboration and dialogue in the digital age. From humble beginnings as alternatives to in-person events to sophisticated virtual experiences enabled by cutting-edge technology, virtual gatherings have become essential tools for diplomatic practice, reshaping the landscape of global diplomacy in profound ways.

5.2 Advantages and Limitations of Virtual Diplomatic Gatherings

Virtual diplomatic gatherings have become increasingly prevalent in the digital age, offering diplomats and policymakers unique opportunities for engagement, collaboration, and dialogue. However, they also present distinct advantages and limitations compared to traditional in-person gatherings. This section explores the advantages and limitations of virtual diplomatic gatherings in the context of contemporary diplomacy.

Advantages:

Accessibility and Inclusivity: Virtual diplomatic gatherings enhance accessibility and inclusivity by eliminating geographical barriers and enabling diplomats from around the world to participate without the need for travel (United Nations Institute for Training and Research, 2019). This facilitates broader participation and representation, particularly for diplomats from developing countries or regions with limited diplomatic resources or infrastructure.

Cost-Effectiveness: Virtual diplomatic gatherings can be more cost-effective than traditional in-person meetings, as they reduce expenses associated with travel, accommodation, and venue rentals (European

External Action Service, 2021). This enables diplomatic institutions to allocate resources more efficiently and maximize their budget for diplomatic initiatives and activities.

Flexibility and Convenience: Virtual diplomatic gatherings offer greater flexibility and convenience for diplomats, allowing them to participate from the comfort of their own offices or homes (Ministry of Foreign Affairs of Denmark, 2020). This flexibility enables diplomats to balance their professional responsibilities with personal commitments and eliminates the logistical challenges associated with travel and accommodation arrangements.

Environmental Sustainability: By reducing the need for travel and minimizing carbon emissions associated with transportation, virtual diplomatic gatherings contribute to environmental sustainability and align with efforts to combat climate change (United Nations Department of Economic and Social Affairs, 2020). This reflects a growing recognition among diplomatic institutions of the importance of adopting environmentally friendly practices in diplomatic operations.

Limitations:

Lack of Personal Interaction: One of the primary limitations of virtual diplomatic gatherings is the absence of personal interaction and face-to-face engagement, which can hinder relationship-building, trust-building, and informal networking opportunities (Council on Foreign Relations, 2020). Non-verbal cues, body language, and interpersonal dynamics may be less apparent in virtual settings, making it challenging to establish rapport and forge meaningful connections.

Technological Challenges: Virtual diplomatic gatherings are susceptible to technological challenges such as internet connectivity issues, software glitches, and compatibility issues with different devices and platforms (European External Action Service, 2021). Technical difficulties can disrupt proceedings, impede communication, and detract from the overall effectiveness of virtual gatherings, particularly in contexts where participants have limited access to reliable technology infrastructure.

Security and Confidentiality Concerns: Virtual diplomatic gatherings raise concerns about data security, confidentiality, and privacy, particularly when sensitive diplomatic discussions or negotiations are conducted online (Council of Europe, 2021). Diplomatic institutions must implement robust cybersecurity measures and encryption protocols to safeguard sensitive information and protect against unauthorized access or cyber threats.

Digital Divide: Despite advancements in technology, a digital divide persists, with disparities in internet access, digital literacy, and technological infrastructure across regions and demographics (United Nations Educational, Scientific and Cultural Organization [UNESCO], 2020). Virtual diplomatic gatherings may exacerbate existing inequalities by excluding diplomats from marginalized communities or countries with limited access to digital resources.

Virtual diplomatic gatherings offer distinct advantages in terms of accessibility, cost-effectiveness, flexibility, and environmental sustainability. However, they also pose challenges related to interpersonal interaction, technological issues, security concerns, and the digital divide. Diplomatic institutions must strike a balance between leveraging the benefits of virtual diplomacy and mitigating its limitations to ensure effective and inclusive diplomatic engagement in the digital age.

5.3 Case Studies: Successful Virtual Summits and Conferences

Several successful case studies illustrate the effectiveness and impact of virtual summits and conferences in diplomatic engagement and collaboration. These case studies showcase innovative approaches, best practices, and lessons learned from virtual gatherings that have yielded positive outcomes in diplomacy.

The Paris Peace Forum, an annual event launched in 2018, has successfully transitioned to a virtual format, bringing together global leaders, policymakers, and civil society representatives to discuss pressing global challenges and propose concrete solutions (Paris Peace Forum, n.d.). Despite the challenges posed by the COVID-19 pandemic, the virtual edition of the forum maintained its momentum and impact, attracting participants from around the world and facilitating meaningful dialogue on issues such as climate change, conflict resolution, and global governance.

The United Nations General Assembly, the largest annual gathering of world leaders, has adapted to virtual platforms to ensure continuity in diplomatic engagement during the COVID-19 pandemic (United Nations, n.d.). The virtual UNGA sessions have provided a platform for heads of state and government to deliver speeches, participate in high-level meetings, and engage in diplomatic discussions on a wide range of global issues. While facing technical challenges and limitations, the virtual UNGA sessions have enabled diplomatic dialogue and decision-making in unprecedented times.

The Munich Security Conference, an annual gathering of policymakers, experts, and stakeholders in international security, successfully transitioned to a virtual format in 2021 (Munich Security Conference, n.d.). The virtual MSC featured interactive panels, virtual networking sessions, and digital exhibits, allowing participants to engage in substantive discussions on pressing security challenges and explore innovative solutions. Despite the absence of face-to-face interactions, the virtual MSC maintained its relevance and impact, fostering dialogue and cooperation on critical security issues.

The African Union (AU) has successfully organized virtual summits and conferences to address regional challenges and promote cooperation among African nations. In response to the COVID-19 pandemic, the AU transitioned its annual summit to a virtual format, allowing heads of state and government from across the continent to participate remotely (African Union Commission, n.d.). The virtual AU summit facilitated discussions on critical issues such as public health, economic recovery, and peace and security, enabling African leaders to coordinate responses to the pandemic and other pressing challenges facing the continent.

These case studies highlight the adaptability and resilience of virtual summits and conferences in diplomatic practice, demonstrating their capacity to facilitate meaningful engagement, collaboration, and decision-making in a digital environment. By leveraging technology and embracing innovative approaches, diplomats and policymakers can harness the potential of virtual platforms to address global challenges, promote international cooperation, and advance diplomatic objectives.

5.4 Future Trends in Virtual Diplomatic Events

The future of virtual diplomatic events is shaped by ongoing technological advancements, changing diplomatic practices, and evolving global challenges. This section explores key trends and developments that are likely to shape the landscape of virtual diplomacy in the years to come, offering insights into emerging opportunities and challenges for diplomats and policymakers.

As the world gradually emerges from the COVID-19 pandemic, hybrid models of diplomatic engagement are expected to gain prominence, combining virtual and in-person elements to maximize accessibility and inclusivity (Slaughter, 2020). Hybrid diplomatic events allow for a combination of virtual participation and physical presence, accommodating diverse preferences and needs while ensuring effective engagement and collaboration among stakeholders.

Technological innovations in virtual collaboration tools are driving the development of more sophisticated and interactive platforms for diplomatic engagement (Fischer et al., 2022). Virtual reality (VR) and augmented reality (AR) technologies offer immersive experiences that simulate real-world interactions, enabling diplomats to engage in virtual meetings, negotiations, and simulations with greater depth and realism. Additionally, advances in artificial intelligence (AI) and natural language processing (NLP) are enhancing the functionality of virtual platforms, enabling real-time translation, transcription, and analysis of diplomatic discussions.

The rise of digital diplomacy and online diplomatic engagement is reshaping the practice of diplomacy, expanding the scope and reach of diplomatic activities beyond traditional channels (Kerr, 2019). Diplomatic missions and organizations are increasingly leveraging social media, digital platforms, and online networks to engage with diverse audiences, communicate policy priorities, and influence public opinion. Digital diplomacy initiatives such as virtual town halls, online forums, and social media campaigns offer diplomats new opportunities for outreach, advocacy, and public diplomacy.

As virtual diplomacy becomes more prevalent, cybersecurity and data privacy considerations are becoming increasingly important (Schmitt, 2017). Diplomatic missions and organizations must prioritize cybersecurity measures to protect sensitive information, secure virtual platforms, and safeguard against cyber threats and attacks. Additionally, concerns about data privacy and digital sovereignty are prompting policymakers to explore strategies for ensuring the integrity and confidentiality of diplomatic communications in the digital realm.

Bridging the digital divide and promoting digital inclusivity are essential for ensuring equitable access to virtual diplomatic events (Morozov, 2020). Efforts to expand global connectivity and improve internet infrastructure in underserved regions are critical for enabling meaningful participation in virtual diplomacy by stakeholders from diverse backgrounds and geographic locations. Diplomatic initiatives that prioritize digital inclusivity and accessibility can help address disparities in access to information and opportunities for engagement in the digital age.

In summary, the future of virtual diplomatic events is characterized by hybrid models of engagement, enhanced virtual collaboration tools, digital diplomacy initiatives, cybersecurity considerations, and efforts to promote global connectivity and digital inclusivity. By embracing these trends and leveraging digital technologies strategically, diplomats and policymakers can enhance diplomatic outcomes, foster international cooperation, and address complex global challenges in the 21st century.

6. Digital Diplomacy in Crisis Management and Humanitarian Assistance

"The internet has democratized diplomacy, allowing citizens to participate in global conversations and influence diplomatic agendas." - Anne-Marie Slaughter

Digital diplomacy has emerged as a critical component in crisis management and humanitarian assistance, revolutionizing traditional diplomatic practices by harnessing digital tools and platforms to facilitate coordination, communication, and response efforts during times of crisis. This chapter delves into the evolving landscape of digital diplomacy in crisis situations, shedding light on its profound impact on humanitarian assistance, disaster response, and conflict resolution.

In today's interconnected world, digital diplomacy serves as a linchpin in crisis management strategies, offering diplomats and policymakers unprecedented opportunities to navigate complex humanitarian challenges with agility and efficacy. By leveraging digital platforms such as social media, messaging apps, and crisis mapping tools, diplomats can swiftly disseminate accurate information, mobilize resources, and coordinate response efforts in real-time (Gruzd & Roy, 2019). These digital channels not only enable diplomats to reach diverse audiences but also empower affected communities to actively participate in the response process, fostering a sense of solidarity and collective action amidst adversity.

Moreover, digital diplomacy plays a pivotal role in facilitating humanitarian assistance and disaster response efforts, transcending geographical barriers to deliver timely aid and support to those in need (Kurbalija, 2018). By leveraging digital platforms for fundraising, crowdfunding, and donation drives, diplomats can mobilize public support and channel resources towards relief operations more effectively. Additionally, digital tools such as crowdsourcing platforms and data analytics enable diplomats and humanitarian organizations to assess needs, map out crisis-affected areas, and coordinate the distribution of aid with precision and efficiency, thereby optimizing the impact of humanitarian interventions.

In the realm of conflict resolution and peacebuilding, digital diplomacy serves as a catalyst for dialogue, reconciliation, and cooperation among conflicting parties (Pascal & Slobodchikoff, 2020). Virtual peace talks, online mediation efforts, and Track II diplomacy initiatives facilitated through digital platforms offer unique opportunities for stakeholders to engage in constructive dialogue and negotiation, transcending political and geographical barriers that often impede traditional diplomacy. By fostering trust-building and confidence-building measures online, diplomats can pave the way for sustainable peace agreements and reconciliation processes in conflict-affected regions, laying the foundation for lasting stability and prosperity.

However, amidst the opportunities presented by digital diplomacy in crisis management and humanitarian assistance, challenges and risks abound (Sevinçli & Özer, 2020). Misinformation and disinformation proliferate on digital platforms, undermining trust and complicating response efforts. Moreover, concerns regarding the digital divide, data privacy, and cybersecurity threaten to exacerbate existing vulnerabilities and inequalities in crisis-affected communities. Diplomats and policymakers must navigate these challenges adeptly, developing strategies to mitigate risks and maximize the potential of digital diplomacy for addressing complex humanitarian challenges and promoting peace and stability in the digital age.

As we look to the future, emerging technologies such as artificial intelligence, blockchain, and virtual reality hold promise for enhancing the effectiveness and efficiency of digital diplomacy efforts in crisis situations (Bjola & Holmes, 2015). By embracing digital innovation, fostering digital literacy, and fostering international cooperation, diplomats can leverage the power of digital diplomacy to navigate the evolving landscape of humanitarian crises and conflict resolution, paving the way for a more resilient and interconnected world.

6.1 The Role of Digital Tools in Crisis Communication and Coordination

Digital tools have revolutionized crisis communication and coordination, offering diplomats and policymakers powerful means to disseminate information, coordinate response efforts, and engage with affected communities during times of crisis. This section delves into the multifaceted role of digital tools in crisis situations, examining their impact on communication, coordination, and community engagement.

In crisis situations, timely and accurate communication is paramount to ensure the safety and well-being of affected populations. Digital tools such as social media platforms, messaging apps, and emergency alert systems serve as vital channels for crisis communication, enabling diplomats to reach diverse audiences instantaneously (Gruzd & Roy, 2019). Through platforms like Twitter, Facebook, and WhatsApp, diplomats can provide real-time updates on developments, share critical information such as evacuation notices and emergency contact information, and dispel rumors and misinformation that may exacerbate panic and confusion.

Furthermore, digital tools facilitate coordination among various stakeholders involved in crisis response efforts, streamlining information sharing, resource mobilization, and collaboration. Platforms like Google Docs, Slack, and Trello allow diplomats and relief organizations to create virtual command centers, where they can centralize information, assign tasks, and track progress in real-time

(Kurbalija, 2018). By leveraging these digital collaboration tools, diplomats can enhance the efficiency and effectiveness of response efforts, ensuring that resources are allocated strategically and response activities are coordinated seamlessly across different agencies and organizations.

Digital tools also empower affected communities to actively participate in crisis response and recovery efforts, fostering a sense of solidarity and resilience amidst adversity. Crisis mapping platforms like Ushahidi and OpenStreetMap enable citizens to report incidents, share information about affected areas, and request assistance in real-time (Meier, 2015). By crowdsourcing information from local communities, diplomats can gain valuable insights into the evolving situation on the ground, identify emerging needs, and tailor response efforts to address specific challenges faced by affected populations.

However, while digital tools offer numerous benefits in crisis communication and coordination, they also present challenges and risks that must be addressed. Misinformation and disinformation spread rapidly on social media platforms, undermining the credibility of official communications and complicating response efforts (Starbird et al., 2014). Diplomats and policymakers must be vigilant in monitoring digital channels, identifying and countering false information, and building trust with affected communities through transparent and accurate communication.

Moreover, concerns regarding data privacy, cybersecurity, and digital literacy pose additional challenges in leveraging digital tools for crisis communication and coordination (Sevinçli & Özer, 2020). Diplomats must prioritize the protection of sensitive information, secure digital platforms against cyber threats, and ensure that affected communities have access to reliable information and resources to navigate the digital landscape safely and effectively.

In conclusion, digital tools play a pivotal role in crisis communication and coordination, enabling diplomats to disseminate information, coordinate response efforts, and engage with affected communities in real-time. By leveraging the power of digital technology responsibly and strategically, diplomats can enhance the effectiveness of crisis response efforts, promote resilience in vulnerable communities, and mitigate the impact of humanitarian crises on a global scale.

6.2 Digital Diplomacy in Humanitarian Aid and Disaster Response

Digital diplomacy plays a pivotal role in facilitating humanitarian aid and disaster response efforts, leveraging digital tools and platforms to mobilize resources, coordinate relief operations, and support affected populations in times of crisis. This section delves into the multifaceted role of digital diplomacy in humanitarian aid and disaster response, examining its impact on fundraising, coordination, and community engagement.

In humanitarian crises and natural disasters, digital diplomacy serves as a powerful tool for raising awareness, mobilizing support, and rallying resources from diverse stakeholders across the globe (Kurbalija, 2018). Digital platforms such as crowdfunding websites, social media campaigns, and online donation portals enable diplomats and relief organizations to appeal for financial assistance and in-kind donations, reaching a wide audience of potential donors and supporters (Cairney & Yamamoto, 2019). By harnessing the power of digital fundraising, diplomats can rapidly mobilize resources to address urgent humanitarian needs and provide critical assistance to affected communities.

Moreover, digital tools facilitate coordination and collaboration among humanitarian actors, streamlining information sharing, logistics management, and resource allocation in complex crisis environments

(Meier, 2015). Platforms like Humanitarian ID, ReliefWeb, and the Digital Humanitarian Network enable diplomats, aid organizations, and volunteers to connect, share data, and coordinate response efforts in real-time (Davies & Jenkins, 2013). By leveraging these digital collaboration platforms, diplomats can optimize the efficiency and effectiveness of humanitarian aid delivery, ensuring that resources are deployed where they are needed most and response activities are coordinated seamlessly across different agencies and organizations.

Digital diplomacy also empowers affected communities to participate in disaster response and recovery efforts, fostering resilience and self-reliance amidst adversity (Meier, 2015). Crisis mapping platforms like Ushahidi and OpenStreetMap enable citizens to report incidents, share information about hazards and resources, and coordinate local response efforts in real-time (Goodchild & Glennon, 2010). By crowdsourcing information from the ground, diplomats can gain valuable insights into the needs and priorities of affected populations, tailor response efforts to address specific challenges, and empower communities to take an active role in their own recovery.

However, while digital diplomacy offers significant opportunities for humanitarian aid and disaster response, it also presents challenges and limitations that must be addressed (Cairney & Yamamoto, 2019). Issues such as digital divide, data privacy concerns, and cybersecurity threats can hinder the effectiveness of digital tools in reaching and assisting vulnerable populations (Sevinçli & Özer, 2020). Diplomats and policymakers must prioritize efforts to bridge the digital divide, protect sensitive information, and ensure the security and integrity of digital platforms to maximize the impact of digital diplomacy in humanitarian crises and disaster situations.

Digital diplomacy plays a crucial role in humanitarian aid and disaster response, enabling diplomats to mobilize resources, coordinate relief efforts, and empower affected communities to participate in their own recovery. By harnessing the power of digital technology responsibly and strategically, diplomats can enhance the effectiveness and efficiency of humanitarian response efforts, mitigate the impact of disasters on vulnerable populations, and promote resilience and self-reliance in crisis-affected communities.

6.3 Conflict Resolution and Peacebuilding Through Digital Diplomacy

Digital diplomacy plays a transformative role in conflict resolution and peacebuilding efforts, leveraging digital tools and platforms to facilitate dialogue, reconciliation, and cooperation among conflicting parties. This section explores the multifaceted role of digital diplomacy in conflict resolution and peacebuilding, examining its impact on virtual negotiations, Track II diplomacy initiatives, and online mediation efforts.

In conflict-affected regions, digital diplomacy offers unique opportunities for diplomats, mediators, and peacebuilders to engage with conflicting parties and foster dialogue in virtual spaces (Pascal & Slobodchikoff, 2020). Virtual peace talks, facilitated through video conferencing platforms and online collaboration tools, enable stakeholders to participate in constructive dialogue and negotiation regardless of geographical barriers or security concerns (Bjola & Holmes, 2015). By providing a neutral and accessible platform for communication, digital diplomacy creates space for conflicting parties to explore common ground, address grievances, and seek mutually acceptable solutions to underlying issues driving conflict.

Moreover, digital tools enable diplomats and mediators to conduct Track II diplomacy initiatives, engaging civil society actors, grassroots organizations, and community leaders in peacebuilding efforts (Kurbalija, 2018). Online forums, virtual workshops, and social media campaigns serve as platforms for dialogue, exchange, and collaboration among diverse stakeholders, amplifying voices that are often marginalized in traditional diplomatic processes (Bjola & Holmes, 2015). By leveraging digital platforms for inclusive and participatory peacebuilding, diplomats can build trust, foster cooperation, and lay the groundwork for sustainable peace agreements that reflect the needs and aspirations of all stakeholders.

Digital diplomacy also facilitates online mediation efforts, allowing third-party mediators and facilitators to intervene in conflicts and facilitate dialogue between conflicting parties (Pascal & Slobodchikoff, 2020). Online mediation platforms, equipped with features such as secure messaging, virtual breakout rooms, and document sharing, enable mediators to conduct confidential and structured negotiations in a virtual environment (Kurbalija, 2018). By providing a safe and neutral space for communication, digital diplomacy enhances the effectiveness of mediation efforts, enabling mediators to bridge divides, manage conflicts, and facilitate the resolution of disputes through dialogue and negotiation.

However, while digital diplomacy offers significant opportunities for conflict resolution and peacebuilding, it also presents challenges and limitations that must be addressed (Sevinçli & Özer, 2020). Issues such as digital divide, cybersecurity threats, and data privacy concerns can undermine the integrity and inclusivity of digital platforms, hindering the effectiveness of digital diplomacy efforts in conflict-affected regions (Bjola & Holmes, 2015). Diplomats and mediators must navigate these challenges adeptly, developing strategies to mitigate risks and leverage digital tools responsibly to advance peace and stability in conflict-affected regions.

Digital diplomacy plays a transformative role in conflict resolution and peacebuilding, offering diplomats, mediators, and peacebuilders powerful means to engage with conflicting parties, foster dialogue, and facilitate cooperation in virtual spaces. By harnessing the power of digital technology strategically and responsibly, diplomats can enhance the effectiveness of peacebuilding efforts, mitigate conflicts, and promote reconciliation and sustainable peace in conflict-affected regions.

6.4 Challenges and Ethical Considerations in Digital Crisis Diplomacy

While digital diplomacy offers numerous opportunities for crisis management and humanitarian assistance, it also presents a myriad of challenges and ethical considerations that must be addressed to maximize its effectiveness and mitigate potential risks. This section delves into the key challenges and ethical considerations in digital crisis diplomacy, examining issues such as misinformation, data privacy, and cybersecurity threats.

One of the primary challenges in digital crisis diplomacy is the proliferation of misinformation and disinformation on digital platforms, which can undermine the credibility of official communications and complicate response efforts (Starbird et al., 2014). In times of crisis, false information spreads rapidly on social media platforms, exacerbating panic and confusion among affected populations. Diplomats and policymakers must be vigilant in monitoring digital channels, identifying and countering false information, and building trust with affected communities through transparent and accurate communication.

Moreover, data privacy concerns pose significant ethical challenges in digital crisis diplomacy, as diplomats and relief organizations collect and use sensitive personal data to coordinate response efforts (Sevinçli & Özer, 2020). In the rush to provide assistance, there is a risk of infringing on individuals' privacy rights and exposing them to potential harm or exploitation. Diplomats must prioritize the protection of sensitive information, adhere to data protection regulations, and ensure that data collection and use are conducted in a transparent and ethical manner.

Additionally, cybersecurity threats loom large in the digital landscape, posing risks to the integrity and security of digital platforms used in crisis diplomacy (Schmitt, 2017). Malicious actors may exploit vulnerabilities in digital systems to disrupt communication, steal sensitive information, or launch cyber attacks against diplomatic missions and relief organizations. Diplomats must implement robust cybersecurity measures to protect digital platforms against threats such as phishing, malware, and distributed denial-of-service (DDoS) attacks, safeguarding the confidentiality, integrity, and availability of critical information and communication channels.

Furthermore, the digital divide exacerbates inequalities in access to information and resources, limiting the effectiveness of digital crisis diplomacy efforts in reaching and assisting vulnerable populations (Cairney & Yamamoto, 2019). In crisis-affected regions with limited internet connectivity or technological infrastructure, marginalized communities may be excluded from digital communication channels, hindering their ability to access timely information, seek assistance, and participate in response efforts. Diplomats and relief organizations must prioritize efforts to bridge the digital divide, ensure equitable access to digital tools and platforms, and empower marginalized communities to engage in digital diplomacy safely and effectively.

Digital crisis diplomacy presents a host of challenges and ethical considerations that diplomats and policymakers must navigate adeptly to maximize its impact and mitigate potential risks. By addressing issues such as misinformation, data privacy, cybersecurity threats, and the digital divide, diplomats can harness the power of digital technology responsibly and ethically to enhance crisis management and humanitarian assistance efforts, promote resilience in vulnerable communities, and foster peace and stability in the face of adversity.

6.5 Innovations and Best Practices in Digital Humanitarian Diplomacy

Digital humanitarian diplomacy continues to evolve rapidly, driven by technological innovations and emerging best practices that enhance the effectiveness and efficiency of humanitarian response efforts. This section explores key innovations and best practices in digital humanitarian diplomacy, highlighting strategies for leveraging digital tools and platforms to address humanitarian challenges and promote resilience in crisis-affected communities.

Crowdsourcing platforms enable diplomats and relief organizations to harness the collective intelligence and resources of online communities to address humanitarian needs (Meier, 2015). By crowdsourcing information, volunteers, and financial contributions, diplomats can mobilize rapid responses to emergencies, identify emerging needs, and engage with affected communities in real-time. Crowdfunding campaigns allow diplomats to raise funds for relief operations, leveraging social media and online platforms to amplify their reach and impact.

Open data initiatives and crisis mapping platforms provide diplomats and relief organizations with valuable information and insights to inform decision-making and prioritize response efforts (Goodchild & Glennon, 2010). By making data on population demographics, infrastructure, and hazards freely available, diplomats can enhance situational awareness, identify vulnerable populations, and target resources more effectively. Crisis mapping platforms enable volunteers to crowdsource information about crisis-affected areas, facilitating the coordination of response efforts and the delivery of aid to those in need.

Digital volunteerism platforms mobilize skilled individuals from around the world to contribute their expertise and resources to humanitarian response efforts (Meier, 2015). Virtual communities of volunteers, such as the Digital Humanitarian Network, collaborate remotely to analyze data, map crises, and provide technical support to relief organizations. By tapping into the collective expertise of digital volunteers, diplomats can augment their capacity to respond to emergencies, innovate new solutions, and build resilience in crisis-affected communities.

Social media platforms offer diplomats and relief organizations powerful tools for engaging with affected communities, raising awareness about humanitarian issues, and advocating for policy change (Cairney & Yamamoto, 2019). Through targeted social media campaigns, diplomats can disseminate information, mobilize public support, and amplify the voices of marginalized communities. Digital advocacy efforts leverage online petitions, hashtags, and viral campaigns to influence policymakers, raise funds, and drive action on humanitarian priorities.

Digital literacy and capacity-building initiatives empower diplomats, relief workers, and local stakeholders to navigate the digital landscape safely and effectively (Kurbalija, 2018). Training programs and workshops provide essential skills in data analysis, social media management, and crisis communication, equipping participants with the knowledge and tools to leverage digital technology for humanitarian purposes. By investing in digital literacy and capacity-building, diplomats can strengthen the resilience of communities, enhance local response capabilities, and foster sustainable development in crisis-affected regions.

Innovations and best practices in digital humanitarian diplomacy offer diplomats and relief organizations powerful means to address humanitarian challenges, promote resilience, and empower communities in crisis-affected regions. By leveraging digital tools and platforms strategically and responsibly, diplomats can enhance the effectiveness and efficiency of humanitarian response efforts, mitigate the impact of disasters on vulnerable populations, and build a more resilient and interconnected world.

6.6 Future Directions

The future of digital diplomacy holds immense potential for innovation, collaboration, and impact in addressing global challenges and promoting international cooperation. This section explores key trends and future directions shaping the evolution of digital diplomacy, highlighting opportunities for diplomats and policymakers to leverage digital technology to advance diplomatic objectives and enhance global governance.

The integration of artificial intelligence (AI) and data analytics into diplomatic practice holds promise for enhancing decision-making, predictive analysis, and policy formulation (Fisher, 2021). AI-powered algorithms can analyze vast amounts of data from diverse sources, uncovering insights, trends, and patterns that inform diplomatic strategies and responses to complex challenges such as climate change, pandemics, and cybersecurity threats. By harnessing the predictive capabilities of AI, diplomats can anticipate emerging trends, identify potential risks, and proactively shape diplomatic agendas to address evolving global dynamics.

Virtual reality (VR) and augmented reality (AR) technologies offer diplomats innovative tools for immersive engagement, cultural exchange, and public diplomacy (Baldwin, 2020). Virtual embassies, cultural exhibitions, and diplomatic simulations conducted in virtual environments enable diplomats to connect with global audiences, showcase cultural heritage, and foster cross-cultural understanding. By harnessing the immersive capabilities of VR and AR, diplomats can transcend geographical barriers, cultivate empathy, and bridge divides between nations and cultures in the digital age.

Blockchain technology holds transformative potential for enhancing transparency, accountability, and trust in diplomatic transactions and international relations (Takagi, 2018). Blockchain-based systems enable secure, tamper-proof record-keeping and verification of diplomatic agreements, treaties, and commitments, reducing the risk of fraud, manipulation, and disputes. Smart contracts powered by blockchain technology automate diplomatic processes, streamline negotiations, and ensure compliance with international agreements, enhancing the efficiency and reliability of diplomatic interactions in a digital environment.

The evolution of digital diplomacy towards multi-stakeholder collaboration and digital governance models fosters inclusive decision-making, citizen engagement, and participatory diplomacy (Chen, 2019). Digital platforms and online forums facilitate dialogue and cooperation among governments, civil society organizations, and private sector actors, enabling stakeholders to collaborate on shared challenges and co-create innovative solutions. By embracing digital governance principles, diplomats can harness the collective wisdom and resources of diverse stakeholders, strengthen international cooperation, and address complex global issues more effectively.

As diplomats increasingly rely on AI-driven technologies for decision-making and analysis, ensuring ethical AI governance and responsible use of AI becomes paramount (Kirkpatrick, 2021). Ethical AI frameworks and guidelines provide diplomats with principles and standards for the development, deployment, and oversight of AI systems in diplomatic practice. By prioritizing transparency, accountability, and human-centric design in AI development, diplomats can uphold ethical standards, mitigate risks, and build trust with stakeholders, ensuring that AI-driven diplomacy advances the common good and upholds democratic values.

The future of digital diplomacy is characterized by innovation, collaboration, and ethical stewardship, offering diplomats unprecedented opportunities to leverage digital technology to address global challenges and promote peace, prosperity, and sustainability. By embracing emerging trends and leveraging digital tools strategically and responsibly, diplomats can shape a more inclusive, resilient, and interconnected world in the digital age.

7. Legal and Ethical Dimensions of Digital Diplomacy

"Digital diplomacy isn't just a tool for communication; it's a platform for building trust and forging meaningful relationships between nations." - Unknown

Digital diplomacy operates within a complex legal and ethical framework, influenced by a dynamic interplay of international law, diplomatic conventions, and the rapid evolution of digital technologies. As diplomats increasingly utilize digital platforms to engage with global audiences and advance diplomatic objectives, it becomes imperative to explore the legal and ethical dimensions underpinning these interactions.

At its core, digital diplomacy intersects with established principles of international law governing diplomatic relations, including the Vienna Convention on Diplomatic Relations and the Vienna Convention on Consular Relations. However, the application of traditional diplomatic norms to digital communication presents novel challenges, such as jurisdictional ambiguity and sovereignty issues in cyberspace (Kirkpatrick, 2021). As diplomats engage in digital interactions across borders, they must grapple with questions of jurisdiction, accountability, and state responsibility in a realm characterized by fluid boundaries and diverse stakeholders.

Moreover, the ethical dimensions of digital diplomacy are multifaceted and require careful consideration in navigating diplomatic engagements online. Data privacy and cybersecurity emerge as paramount ethical concerns, as diplomats handle sensitive information and communicate through digital channels vulnerable to cyber threats (Sevinçli & Özer, 2020). Diplomats must uphold ethical principles of transparency, accountability, and integrity in their handling of digital data, ensuring that diplomatic communications and negotiations are conducted securely and ethically.

Freedom of expression is another ethical principle that intersects with digital diplomacy, as diplomats engage with diverse audiences and communicate policy messages through digital platforms (Cairney & Yamamoto, 2019). Diplomats must safeguard the right to freedom of expression while also balancing the need to maintain diplomatic decorum and protect national interests. This requires diplomats to exercise discretion, sensitivity, and ethical judgment in their digital communications, fostering open dialogue while guarding against hate speech, disinformation, and incitement to violence.

Furthermore, ethical AI governance emerges as a critical consideration in digital diplomacy, as diplomats increasingly rely on AI-driven technologies for decision-making and analysis (Kirkpatrick, 2021). Diplomats must ensure that AI systems uphold ethical standards, respect human rights, and promote transparency, accountability, and fairness in diplomatic practice. By prioritizing ethical AI governance, diplomats can harness the potential of AI to enhance diplomatic effectiveness while mitigating risks and safeguarding against unintended consequences.

Digital diplomacy operates within a complex legal and ethical terrain, shaped by international law, diplomatic norms, and the evolving dynamics of digital technology. By navigating these challenges with diligence, integrity, and ethical awareness, diplomats and policymakers can leverage digital diplomacy to advance global cooperation, promote peace and stability, and uphold democratic values in the digital age.

7.1 International Law and Digital Diplomacy

Digital diplomacy operates within the established framework of international law, which encompasses a rich tapestry of treaties, conventions, and customary norms governing diplomatic interactions and relations between states (Wouters & Defraigne, 2020). Central to this legal landscape are cornerstone agreements such as the Vienna Convention on Diplomatic Relations (1961) and the Vienna Convention on Consular Relations (1963), which lay down foundational principles regarding diplomatic immunity, privileges, and obligations. These conventions provide a bedrock for diplomatic practice, establishing norms that have guided diplomatic conduct for decades.

However, the rapid evolution of digital communication technologies has introduced novel challenges to the application of traditional diplomatic norms. In the borderless expanse of cyberspace, jurisdictional boundaries become blurred, raising complex questions about sovereignty, jurisdiction, and state responsibility (Kirkpatrick, 2021). Unlike physical territories, cyberspace transcends geographical limitations, presenting diplomats with unique legal complexities when conducting digital communications and engagements.

Diplomats must adeptly navigate these legal intricacies, balancing adherence to established international law with the innovative use of digital technology to advance diplomatic objectives and promote international cooperation. This requires diplomats to remain informed about developments in international law relevant to cyberspace and to collaborate with legal experts to interpret and apply legal norms effectively in the digital realm.

Moreover, the emergence of cyber threats such as hacking, cyber espionage, and cyber warfare further complicates the legal landscape of digital diplomacy. Diplomats must remain vigilant in addressing these security challenges while upholding principles of international law and respecting the sovereignty and territorial integrity of states.

In summary, digital diplomacy operates within the framework of international law, guided by treaties, conventions, and customary norms that govern diplomatic interactions. While the borderless nature of cyberspace presents challenges to the application of traditional diplomatic norms, diplomats must navigate these legal complexities with skill and diligence, ensuring that digital diplomacy remains rooted in the principles of international law and contributes to the promotion of peace, stability, and cooperation in the digital age.

7.2 Data Privacy and Cybersecurity

Data privacy and cybersecurity are paramount ethical considerations in the practice of digital diplomacy, given the sensitive nature of information handled by diplomats and the inherent vulnerabilities of digital communication channels (Sevinçli & Özer, 2020). Diplomats must place a premium on protecting personal data and ensuring compliance with data protection regulations to safeguard the privacy rights of individuals involved in diplomatic communications.

Adherence to robust cybersecurity measures is essential to mitigate the risk of cyber threats such as hacking, espionage, and other malicious activities that pose significant risks to diplomatic communications and national security (Schmitt, 2017). Diplomats must implement comprehensive cybersecurity protocols to fortify digital platforms against potential breaches, ensuring the integrity, confidentiality, and availability of sensitive information.

In addition to technical safeguards, diplomats must uphold ethical principles of transparency, accountability, and integrity in their handling of digital data. Transparency entails providing clear and accessible information to stakeholders about data collection, processing, and storage practices, fostering trust and confidence in diplomatic engagements. Accountability requires diplomats to assume responsibility for the security and integrity of digital data entrusted to them, acknowledging their duty to safeguard sensitive information from unauthorized access or disclosure. Integrity demands honesty, fairness, and adherence to ethical standards in the conduct of diplomatic communications and negotiations, ensuring that diplomatic activities are conducted in a manner consistent with ethical norms and principles.

By prioritizing data privacy and cybersecurity and upholding ethical principles in their handling of digital data, diplomats can promote trust, accountability, and integrity in digital diplomacy, fostering secure and reliable diplomatic engagements that uphold the rights and interests of all stakeholders involved.

7.3 Freedom of Expression and Digital Diplomacy

Freedom of expression is a cornerstone of democratic societies and a fundamental human right that lies at the intersection of digital diplomacy. As diplomats increasingly utilize digital platforms to engage with global audiences and convey policy messages, they must uphold principles of freedom of expression while navigating the complexities of digital communication (Cairney & Yamamoto, 2019).

Diplomats play a crucial role in promoting open dialogue and respecting diverse perspectives in digital spaces. By engaging with audiences from different cultural backgrounds and ideological viewpoints, diplomats can foster mutual understanding, build bridges between nations, and promote cooperation on shared challenges. Upholding freedom of expression requires diplomats to create an environment conducive to respectful discourse, where individuals feel empowered to express their opinions and engage in constructive dialogue.

However, freedom of expression must be balanced with the need to maintain diplomatic decorum and protect national interests. Diplomats must exercise discretion, sensitivity, and ethical judgment in their digital communications to avoid inadvertently causing offense or exacerbating tensions. This requires diplomats to carefully consider the potential impact of their words and actions on diplomatic relations and global perceptions.

Moreover, diplomats must be vigilant in safeguarding against hate speech, disinformation, and incitement to violence in digital spaces. In an era of rampant misinformation and online extremism, diplomats have a responsibility to counter harmful narratives and promote fact-based discourse. By combatting hate speech and disinformation, diplomats can contribute to a safer, more inclusive online environment that upholds democratic values and respects human dignity.

In summary, freedom of expression is a fundamental principle that underpins digital diplomacy, enabling diplomats to engage with diverse audiences and promote open dialogue in digital spaces. By upholding principles of freedom of expression while exercising discretion and ethical judgment, diplomats can navigate the complexities of digital communication and advance diplomatic objectives in an increasingly interconnected world.

7.4 Ethical AI Governance in Diplomacy

The integration of artificial intelligence (AI) into digital diplomacy brings forth a host of ethical considerations that diplomats must grapple with as they navigate the evolving landscape of diplomatic practice (Kirkpatrick, 2021). While AI offers tremendous potential to streamline decision-making processes, optimize analysis, and automate routine tasks, its deployment also raises ethical challenges related to transparency, accountability, and fairness.

Ethical AI governance frameworks play a crucial role in guiding diplomats in the responsible development, deployment, and use of AI technologies in diplomatic practice. These frameworks provide diplomats with guidelines and principles to ensure that AI systems uphold ethical standards, respect human rights, and promote transparency and accountability in decision-making processes.

Key considerations within ethical AI governance frameworks include:

Transparency: Diplomats must ensure transparency in the development and deployment of AI systems, providing clear explanations of how AI algorithms function and the data sources they rely on. Transparent AI systems enable stakeholders to understand the rationale behind decisions and hold diplomats accountable for their actions.

Accountability: Diplomats are accountable for the decisions made by AI systems under their purview. Establishing mechanisms for accountability ensures that diplomats take responsibility for the outcomes of AI-driven decisions and take corrective action when necessary.

Fairness: AI systems must be designed and deployed in a manner that promotes fairness and mitigates bias. Diplomats must carefully consider the potential biases embedded in AI algorithms and take steps to address them to ensure equitable outcomes for all stakeholders.

Human Rights: AI systems should respect and uphold human rights principles, including privacy, freedom of expression, and non-discrimination. Diplomats must ensure that AI technologies are used in a manner that respects the dignity and rights of individuals affected by their decisions.

Risk Mitigation: Diplomats must proactively identify and mitigate risks associated with AI deployment, including unintended consequences, security vulnerabilities, and ethical dilemmas. Robust risk assessment processes enable diplomats to anticipate and address potential harms before they arise.

By prioritizing ethical AI governance, diplomats can harness the potential of AI to enhance diplomatic effectiveness while safeguarding against the risks and ethical pitfalls associated with its deployment. Ethical AI governance frameworks provide diplomats with the tools and principles necessary to navigate the ethical complexities of AI-driven diplomacy and uphold the values of transparency, accountability, and fairness in diplomatic practice.

7.5 Transparency and Accountability

Transparency and accountability serve as cornerstones of effective digital diplomacy, enabling diplomats to foster trust and credibility in their interactions with diverse stakeholders (Chen, 2019). By upholding principles of transparency and providing accurate and timely information to the public, diplomats can enhance public understanding of diplomatic initiatives and promote engagement in diplomatic processes.

Transparency entails openness and accessibility in diplomatic communication, ensuring that information about diplomatic activities, policies, and decisions is readily available to stakeholders. Diplomats must provide clear explanations of their objectives, priorities, and actions, enabling stakeholders to understand the rationale behind diplomatic initiatives and participate meaningfully in decision-making processes. Open dialogue with stakeholders through digital platforms facilitates transparency, allowing diplomats to solicit feedback, address concerns, and build consensus around diplomatic initiatives.

Accountability complements transparency by ensuring that diplomats are held responsible for their actions and decisions. Diplomats must adhere to ethical standards of integrity, honesty, and impartiality in their digital communications and interactions, demonstrating a commitment to professionalism and ethical conduct. By holding themselves accountable for their actions, diplomats earn the trust and confidence of stakeholders, strengthening the legitimacy of diplomatic efforts and promoting public confidence in diplomatic institutions.

Furthermore, diplomats must engage in open dialogue with stakeholders to foster trust and accountability in diplomatic practice. By soliciting feedback, addressing concerns, and seeking input from diverse perspectives, diplomats can demonstrate a commitment to inclusivity and responsiveness, enhancing the legitimacy and effectiveness of diplomatic initiatives. Openness to dialogue and collaboration enables diplomats to build constructive relationships with stakeholders, fostering mutual understanding and cooperation in pursuit of shared goals.

Transparency and accountability are essential principles that underpin effective digital diplomacy. By upholding these principles, diplomats can foster trust, credibility, and legitimacy in their interactions with stakeholders, promoting public confidence in diplomatic institutions and facilitating meaningful engagement in diplomatic processes.

7.6 Ethical Considerations in Online Diplomatic Engagement

Ethical considerations play a crucial role in guiding diplomats' conduct and decision-making in online diplomatic engagement, shaping the norms and practices that govern digital diplomacy. As diplomats navigate the complexities of the digital age, they must uphold ethical principles that promote integrity, transparency, accountability, and respect for human rights.

Integrity: Diplomats must maintain the highest standards of integrity in their online interactions, adhering to ethical norms and principles that govern diplomatic conduct. This includes acting with honesty, fairness, and impartiality in their communications and engagements, avoiding conflicts of interest, and upholding the dignity and reputation of diplomatic institutions.

Transparency: Transparency is essential in online diplomatic engagement, as diplomats communicate with diverse stakeholders through digital platforms. Diplomats must provide accurate and timely information to the public, ensuring transparency in the decision-making process and fostering trust and confidence in diplomatic initiatives.

Accountability: Diplomats are accountable for their actions and decisions in online diplomatic engagement. They must take responsibility for the outcomes of their digital interactions, acknowledge mistakes, and take corrective action when necessary. By holding themselves accountable, diplomats demonstrate a commitment to ethical conduct and uphold the credibility of diplomatic institutions.

Respect for Human Rights: Diplomats must respect and uphold human rights principles in their online engagement, including the right to freedom of expression, privacy, and non-discrimination. Diplomatic activities should not infringe upon individuals' rights and freedoms, and diplomats should work to promote and protect human rights in their digital interactions.

Cultural Sensitivity: Diplomats must demonstrate cultural sensitivity and awareness in their online engagement, respecting diverse perspectives, values, and traditions. Cultural sensitivity fosters mutual understanding and cooperation in digital diplomacy, enabling diplomats to bridge cultural divides and build constructive relationships with stakeholders from different backgrounds.

Professionalism: Diplomats should maintain professionalism in their online interactions, adhering to codes of conduct and diplomatic protocols that govern diplomatic practice. Professionalism entails treating others with respect, conducting oneself with dignity and decorum, and representing one's country or organization in a positive and professional manner.

By upholding these ethical considerations in online diplomatic engagement, diplomats can contribute to the promotion of peace, cooperation, and understanding in the digital age, fostering trust and credibility in diplomatic relations and advancing shared goals and interests on the global stage.

7.7 Future Legal and Ethical Challenges in Digital Diplomacy

Anticipating future legal and ethical challenges is crucial for diplomats and policymakers as they navigate the evolving landscape of digital diplomacy. Several key challenges are likely to emerge in the years ahead:

Data Privacy and Security: With the increasing digitization of diplomatic activities, diplomats must grapple with the protection of sensitive information and the privacy rights of individuals. Ensuring robust data privacy measures and cybersecurity protocols will be essential to mitigate the risk of data breaches and unauthorized access to diplomatic communications.

Regulation of Digital Platforms: Diplomatic engagement often occurs through third-party digital platforms, raising questions about their regulation and accountability. Diplomats may face challenges in navigating the diverse legal frameworks governing digital platforms and ensuring compliance with relevant regulations while maintaining diplomatic independence and freedom of expression.

AI Governance: The growing reliance on artificial intelligence (AI) technologies in diplomatic decision-making poses ethical challenges related to bias, accountability, and transparency. Diplomats must grapple with the development of ethical AI governance frameworks that ensure the responsible use of AI while upholding human rights and democratic values.

Cybersecurity Threats: The proliferation of cyber threats such as hacking, cyber espionage, and disinformation campaigns poses significant challenges to digital diplomacy. Diplomats will need to strengthen cybersecurity defenses, enhance threat intelligence capabilities, and collaborate with international partners to address emerging cyber threats effectively.

Digital Divide: Access to digital technologies remains uneven globally, creating disparities in digital diplomacy capabilities and exacerbating existing inequalities in diplomatic engagement. Diplomats must address the digital divide by promoting digital literacy, expanding access to technology, and ensuring inclusive participation in digital diplomacy initiatives.

Ethical Use of Social Media: Diplomats' use of social media platforms for diplomatic communication raises ethical considerations related to transparency, authenticity, and accountability. Diplomats will need to develop guidelines and best practices for ethical social media engagement, balancing the benefits of digital diplomacy with the risks of misinformation and online abuse.

Addressing these future legal and ethical challenges will require proactive measures, collaboration between governments and technology companies, and ongoing dialogue among stakeholders. By staying ahead of emerging trends and developments in digital diplomacy, diplomats can effectively navigate the complexities of the digital age and advance diplomatic objectives in a rapidly evolving global landscape.

8. Diplomatic Training and Capacity Building in the Digital Age

"In the digital realm, diplomats must be fluent not only in the language of their counterparts but also in the language of algorithms and analytics." - Richard Stengel

Digital age has not merely brought incremental changes but has fundamentally reshaped the landscape of diplomatic practice. Diplomats and Foreign Service professionals are confronted with a paradigm shift that demands a reevaluation of traditional approaches and the acquisition of new skills. With emerging technologies continually reshaping communication channels, information dissemination, and global interactions, diplomats must adapt swiftly to these changes to remain effective in their roles (Bryant & Holt, 2020).

This chapter delves into the critical importance of diplomatic training and capacity building in light of these transformations. It underscores the necessity for diplomats to cultivate a comprehensive understanding of digital tools, platforms, and strategies to navigate the complexities of the modern diplomatic landscape. As the digital realm becomes increasingly intertwined with diplomatic activities, diplomats must be equipped with the knowledge, competencies, and tools necessary to harness the potential of digital technology effectively (Kurbalija, 2018).

The significance of diplomatic training in the digital age lies in its role as a catalyst for empowerment and adaptation. Diplomatic training programs serve as incubators for innovation and resilience, offering diplomats the opportunity to acquire the requisite skills and expertise to thrive in a rapidly evolving environment. By examining strategies for equipping diplomats with digital literacy, technological proficiency, and strategic communication skills, this chapter seeks to illuminate pathways for diplomats to leverage digital technology as a force multiplier in advancing diplomatic objectives on the global stage (Melissen, 2015).

In essence, diplomatic training and capacity building in the digital age are not merely a matter of convenience but a strategic imperative for diplomats and foreign service professionals. By embracing the transformative potential of digital technology and investing in continuous learning and skill development, diplomats can enhance their effectiveness, agility, and relevance in an increasingly interconnected and dynamic world.

8.1 Integrating Digital Skills into Diplomatic Training Programs

In response to the transformative impact of the digital age on diplomatic practice, it is imperative for diplomatic training programs to evolve and integrate digital skills into their curriculum. This section highlights the importance of incorporating digital skills training into diplomatic education and explores strategies for effectively integrating these skills into training programs.

Digital skills encompass a broad range of competencies, including digital literacy, data analysis, cybersecurity, social media management, and emerging technologies such as artificial intelligence and blockchain. Diplomatic training programs must prioritize the development of these skills to equip diplomats with the tools and knowledge needed to thrive in the digital age.

One approach to integrating digital skills into diplomatic training programs is through dedicated modules or courses focused on digital diplomacy and technology-enabled diplomacy. These modules can cover topics such as the role of social media in diplomacy, digital communication strategies, online diplomacy tools, and the ethical implications of digital diplomacy.

In addition to standalone courses, digital skills can also be integrated into existing courses across various subjects, such as negotiation, conflict resolution, and public diplomacy. For example, diplomats can learn how to leverage digital tools for conflict analysis and resolution, use data analytics to inform diplomatic decision-making, and harness social media for public engagement and advocacy.

Furthermore, diplomatic training programs can incorporate practical exercises, case studies, and simulations to provide hands-on experience with digital tools and technologies. Diplomats can engage in mock diplomatic negotiations conducted in virtual environments, analyze real-world diplomatic challenges using data-driven approaches, and develop digital communication campaigns to address pressing international issues.

Collaboration with technology experts, academic institutions, and private sector partners can also enhance diplomatic training programs by providing access to cutting-edge knowledge and expertise in digital technology. Guest lectures, workshops, and joint research projects can enrich diplomats' understanding of emerging technologies and their applications in diplomatic practice.

Ultimately, integrating digital skills into diplomatic training programs is essential to ensure that diplomats are equipped to navigate the complexities of the modern diplomatic landscape. By fostering digital literacy, technological proficiency, and innovation, diplomatic training programs can empower diplomats to effectively leverage digital technology to advance diplomatic objectives and address global challenges in an increasingly interconnected world.

8.2 Case Studies: Innovative Approaches to Diplomatic Capacity Building

This section presents case studies that highlight innovative approaches to diplomatic capacity building in the digital age. These case studies showcase how diplomatic institutions and organizations have adapted their training programs to equip diplomats with the skills, knowledge, and tools needed to thrive in an increasingly digital world.

The Digital Diplomacy Academy, established by a coalition of diplomatic institutions and academic partners, offers a comprehensive online training program focused on digital diplomacy and technology-enabled diplomacy. The academy provides diplomats with access to interactive courses, webinars, and workshops covering a wide range of topics, including social media management, cybersecurity, data analytics, and virtual negotiations (Smith, 2020). Through a combination of self-paced learning modules and live training sessions, diplomats gain practical skills and insights into the latest trends and best practices in digital diplomacy.

Several diplomatic institutions have embraced virtual reality (VR) technology as a tool for immersive diplomatic training. By leveraging VR simulations and scenarios, diplomats can engage in realistic diplomatic exercises, such as crisis management simulations, diplomatic negotiations, and cultural exchanges, in virtual environments (United Nations Institute for Training and Research, 2019). These VR training programs offer diplomats the opportunity to hone their diplomatic skills, enhance cross-cultural communication, and experience high-pressure diplomatic scenarios in a safe and controlled environment.

Hackathons, collaborative events where programmers, designers, and subject matter experts come together to develop innovative solutions to specific challenges, have emerged as a novel approach to diplomatic capacity building. Diplomatic institutions organize hackathons focused on diplomatic challenges, such as public diplomacy campaigns, crisis response strategies, and digital innovation in diplomacy (Diplomatic Courier, 2018). Diplomats collaborate with technologists, entrepreneurs, and civil society actors to develop creative solutions using digital technology, fostering cross-sectoral collaboration and innovation in diplomatic practice.

Data diplomacy workshops provide diplomats with training in data analysis, visualization, and interpretation to inform diplomatic decision-making and policy formulation. Diplomatic institutions partner with data analytics experts and academic institutions to deliver workshops that cover topics such as data sourcing, data-driven diplomacy, and the ethical use of data in diplomatic practice (Council on Foreign Relations, 2020). Diplomats learn how to leverage data analytics tools and techniques to analyze complex diplomatic issues, identify trends and patterns, and develop evidence-based policy recommendations.

Diplomatic institutions organize digital skills exchanges where diplomats from different countries come together to share best practices, experiences, and lessons learned in digital diplomacy and technology-enabled diplomacy. Through workshops, peer-to-peer learning sessions, and collaborative projects, diplomats exchange insights into effective digital communication strategies, social media engagement tactics, and innovative uses of technology in diplomacy (European External Action Service, 2021). Digital skills exchanges promote cross-cultural learning and collaboration, fostering a global community of digitally savvy diplomats.

These case studies illustrate the diverse approaches to diplomatic capacity building in the digital age, highlighting the importance of innovation, collaboration, and adaptation in equipping diplomats with the skills and knowledge needed to navigate the complexities of contemporary diplomacy.

8.3 The Role of Digital Literacy in Enhancing Diplomatic Effectiveness

Digital literacy, encompassing the ability to access, evaluate, and utilize digital information effectively, plays a pivotal role in enhancing diplomatic effectiveness in the digital age. This section examines how diplomats' proficiency in digital literacy contributes to their ability to navigate the complexities of contemporary diplomacy and achieve diplomatic objectives.

Information Management: Diplomats must sift through vast amounts of digital information from diverse sources, ranging from official documents to social media posts, to stay informed about international developments and trends. Digital literacy enables diplomats to discern credible sources, analyze data, and synthesize information to make informed decisions and formulate diplomatic strategies (Cornell University Library, 2021). By effectively managing digital information, diplomats can enhance their situational awareness, anticipate emerging challenges, and identify opportunities for diplomatic engagement.

Communication and Engagement: In the digital age, communication has become increasingly decentralized and mediated through digital platforms such as social media, email, and instant messaging. Diplomats' proficiency in digital literacy enables them to communicate effectively across digital channels, engage with diverse stakeholders, and amplify their diplomatic messages to broader audiences (Ministry of Foreign Affairs of Denmark, 2020). By leveraging digital communication tools strategically, diplomats can foster dialogue, build relationships, and shape public perceptions to advance diplomatic objectives.

Public Diplomacy and Soft Power: Digital literacy is essential for diplomats engaged in public diplomacy efforts aimed at influencing foreign public opinion and projecting soft power. Diplomats proficient in digital literacy can leverage social media, digital storytelling, and online engagement tactics to craft compelling narratives, disseminate cultural and political messages, and build positive relationships with foreign audiences (Melissen, 2015). By harnessing the power of digital platforms, diplomats can enhance their country's image, promote cultural exchange, and strengthen diplomatic ties with partner countries.

Crisis Management and Response: In times of crisis, digital literacy is crucial for diplomats tasked with managing communication, coordination, and response efforts. Diplomats proficient in digital literacy can leverage social media monitoring tools, crisis communication protocols, and digital platforms to disseminate timely information, coordinate international assistance, and address misinformation and disinformation (United Nations Department of Economic and Social Affairs, 2020). By effectively utilizing digital technology, diplomats can mitigate the impact of crises, build resilience in affected communities, and foster international cooperation in crisis response efforts.

Data Analysis and Diplomatic Decision-Making: Digital literacy empowers diplomats to harness the power of data analytics and technology-driven insights to inform diplomatic decision-making. Diplomats proficient in digital literacy can analyze big data, conduct sentiment analysis, and leverage predictive analytics to identify trends, assess risks, and develop evidence-based policy recommendations (Council on Foreign Relations, 2020). By integrating data-driven insights into diplomatic practice, diplomats can enhance their strategic foresight, anticipate diplomatic challenges, and optimize resource allocation to achieve diplomatic objectives.

Digital literacy is indispensable for diplomats seeking to navigate the complexities of contemporary diplomacy and achieve diplomatic effectiveness in the digital age. By enhancing their proficiency in digital literacy, diplomats can strengthen their information management capabilities, communication skills, public diplomacy efforts, crisis management readiness, and data-driven decision-making, ultimately advancing their country's diplomatic interests and promoting international cooperation and understanding.

8.4 Challenges and Opportunities in Digital Diplomatic Education

Digital diplomatic education presents both challenges and opportunities as diplomatic institutions adapt to the demands of the digital age. This section examines the key challenges facing digital diplomatic education and explores the opportunities for innovation and enhancement in this field.

Challenges:

Access and Inclusivity: One of the primary challenges in digital diplomatic education is ensuring equitable access to training programs and resources for diplomats worldwide. Disparities in internet access, technological infrastructure, and digital literacy may hinder diplomats from less developed regions from fully participating in digital training initiatives (United Nations Educational, Scientific and Cultural Organization [UNESCO], 2020). Bridging the digital divide and promoting inclusivity in digital diplomatic education require proactive measures to address infrastructure gaps and provide targeted support to underrepresented groups.

Quality and Relevance: Maintaining the quality and relevance of digital diplomatic education programs is another challenge, given the rapid pace of technological advancement and evolving diplomatic practices. Diplomatic training content must be continuously updated to reflect emerging trends, best practices, and geopolitical developments (Smith, 2020). Ensuring that digital training programs meet the diverse needs and preferences of diplomats from different cultural and professional backgrounds is essential for enhancing their effectiveness and impact.

Cybersecurity and Privacy Concerns: Digital diplomatic education raises concerns about cybersecurity and privacy, particularly regarding the protection of sensitive diplomatic information and personal data. Diplomatic institutions must implement robust cybersecurity measures to safeguard training platforms, communication channels, and digital assets from cyber threats and attacks (Council of Europe, 2021). Respecting diplomats' privacy rights and adhering to data protection regulations are also paramount to maintaining trust and integrity in digital diplomatic education initiatives.

Opportunities:

Flexibility and Adaptability: Digital diplomatic education offers unprecedented flexibility and adaptability, enabling diplomats to access training resources anytime, anywhere, and at their own pace. Online learning platforms, webinars, and virtual classrooms provide diplomats with opportunities for continuous learning and professional development without geographical constraints (European External Action Service [EEAS], 2021). Leveraging digital technology allows diplomatic institutions to tailor training programs to diplomats' individual needs and preferences, enhancing their learning experience and engagement.

Digital diplomatic education fosters innovation and collaboration among diplomatic institutions, academic partners, and technology providers. Virtual reality simulations, gamified learning modules, and interactive multimedia resources offer immersive and engaging learning experiences for diplomats (Ministry of Foreign Affairs of Japan, 2019). Collaborative initiatives such as joint training programs, knowledge-sharing networks, and virtual exchanges enable diplomats to learn from diverse perspectives, exchange best practices, and build networks of professional contacts across borders.

Digital diplomatic education generates valuable data and insights that can inform program evaluation, curriculum development, and strategic planning. Analyzing learning analytics, user feedback, and performance metrics enables diplomatic institutions to assess the effectiveness and impact of training programs, identify areas for improvement, and optimize resource allocation (UNESCO, 2020). Data-driven decision-making enhances the accountability, transparency, and quality of digital diplomatic education initiatives, ensuring their long-term sustainability and relevance.

Digital diplomatic education presents both challenges and opportunities for diplomats and diplomatic institutions. By addressing access barriers, ensuring quality and relevance, addressing cybersecurity concerns, leveraging flexibility and adaptability, fostering innovation and collaboration, and embracing data-driven insights and evaluation, diplomatic institutions can maximize the benefits of digital technology in enhancing diplomats' skills, knowledge, and effectiveness in the digital age.

Part II
Advancing Diplomacy in Key Sectors

9. The Role of Digital Diplomacy in Economic Diplomacy

"Digital diplomacy facilitates real-time communication and information sharing, enabling governments to navigate complex economic landscapes and forge strategic alliances in the digital realm." - Corneliu Bjola

Digital diplomacy, a contemporary manifestation of diplomatic engagement facilitated by digital technologies, has emerged as a crucial tool in the realm of economic diplomacy. Economic diplomacy, traditionally focused on negotiating trade agreements and fostering economic relationships between nations, has been significantly transformed by the advent of digital platforms and communication channels. In recent years, the role of digital diplomacy in economic diplomacy has become increasingly prominent, as it enables governments to engage in real-time communication, negotiate agreements, and address economic issues on a global scale.

One key aspect of digital diplomacy in economic diplomacy is its ability to facilitate communication and information exchange between governments, businesses, and international organizations. Through social media platforms, official government websites, and virtual conferences, diplomats can engage with counterparts from other nations to discuss trade policies, investment opportunities, and economic partnerships. For instance, a study by Smith (2020) highlighted how Twitter has become a significant platform for diplomats to communicate directly with citizens and businesses, disseminating information about economic policies and promoting their country's economic interests.

Moreover, digital diplomacy has also revolutionized the way economic data is analyzed and utilized in diplomatic negotiations. With the vast amount of data available online, diplomats can access real-time economic indicators, market trends, and trade statistics to inform their negotiating positions. This accessibility to data allows diplomats to craft more informed and strategic economic policies, ultimately enhancing their country's economic diplomacy efforts. As noted by Johnson and Lee (2019), digital platforms such as data visualization tools and economic databases play a crucial role in helping diplomats understand complex economic issues and formulate effective strategies.

Furthermore, digital diplomacy serves as a catalyst for promoting economic cooperation and innovation between nations. By leveraging digital platforms, governments can collaborate on joint research projects, innovation initiatives, and technology transfers, fostering economic growth and development. For example, through digital channels, governments can facilitate partnerships between academic institutions, research centers, and businesses to promote technology exchange and entrepreneurship. This collaborative approach to economic diplomacy not only enhances economic ties between nations but also promotes innovation and sustainable development (Lee & Smith, 2021).

The role of digital diplomacy in economic diplomacy is paramount in today's interconnected world. By leveraging digital technologies, diplomats can enhance communication, access real-time data, and promote collaboration to advance economic interests on a global scale. As digital diplomacy continues to evolve, its impact on economic diplomacy will likely become even more profound, shaping the future of international economic relations and cooperation.

9.1. Digital Trade and Economic Agreements

In today's interconnected world, digital trade has emerged as a cornerstone of economic activity, shaping the way businesses operate and nations engage in commerce. The rapid proliferation of digital technologies has revolutionized traditional trade practices, enabling companies to transcend geographical boundaries and tap into global markets with unprecedented ease. As such, policymakers are increasingly recognizing the significance of digital trade in fostering economic growth and innovation. Consequently, a new era of economic agreements tailored to the digital landscape has emerged, aimed at addressing the unique challenges and opportunities presented by the digital economy.

One of the pivotal aspects of digital trade agreements is their emphasis on facilitating cross-border data flows. Data has become the lifeblood of the modern economy, driving innovation, powering digital services, and enhancing productivity. Therefore, ensuring the seamless movement of data across borders is essential for businesses to thrive in today's digital ecosystem. Digital trade agreements, such as the Comprehensive and Progressive Agreement for Trans-Pacific Partnership (CPTPP), include provisions that promote the free flow of data while safeguarding individuals' privacy and data protection rights (Government of Canada, 2020). By establishing clear rules for data governance and cross-border data transfers, these agreements provide businesses with the certainty and confidence needed to invest in digital technologies and expand their global reach.

Moreover, digital trade agreements play a crucial role in addressing emerging challenges such as digital piracy, cybercrime, and intellectual property rights protection. The proliferation of digital technologies has created new avenues for illicit activities, posing significant risks to businesses and consumers alike. To combat these threats, digital trade agreements incorporate robust enforcement mechanisms and intellectual property provisions to safeguard the interests of right holders and promote a level playing field for businesses (World Trade Organization, 2020). By strengthening intellectual property rights protection and enhancing cooperation on cybersecurity, these agreements foster a secure and conducive environment for digital trade to flourish.

Furthermore, digital trade agreements serve as a catalyst for fostering digital inclusion and bridging the digital divide. While digital technologies offer immense opportunities for economic development, disparities in access to technology and digital skills remain a challenge, particularly in developing countries. Digital trade agreements recognize the importance of bridging this gap and promote capacity-building initiatives to enable all countries to harness the benefits of the digital economy (United Nations Conference on Trade and Development, 2020). Through targeted assistance programs and technology transfer initiatives, these agreements empower developing countries to participate more actively in global digital trade, thereby contributing to inclusive and sustainable economic growth.

In conclusion, digital trade agreements represent a crucial framework for navigating the complexities of the digital economy and shaping the future of global commerce. By promoting the free flow of data, enhancing intellectual property rights protection, and fostering digital inclusion, these agreements lay the groundwork for a more prosperous and equitable digital future. As technology continues to evolve and reshape the global economy, digital trade agreements will remain essential instruments for promoting innovation, driving economic growth, and advancing shared prosperity on a global scale.

9.2. Investment Promotion through Digital Channels

In today's interconnected world, digital trade has become an indispensable component of global commerce, fostering economic growth and innovation across borders. As countries strive to harness the potential of digital technologies, the negotiation and implementation of effective economic agreements have emerged as pivotal mechanisms for facilitating digital trade. According to Smith (2020), digital trade encompasses a broad spectrum of activities, including the exchange of digital goods and services, cross-border data flows, and electronic transactions. This paradigm shift in trade dynamics necessitates the adaptation of traditional trade frameworks to accommodate the unique challenges and opportunities presented by the digital economy.

One of the primary objectives of digital trade agreements is to establish a conducive regulatory environment that promotes innovation while safeguarding consumer privacy and data security (Jones, 2019). For instance, provisions related to intellectual property rights and e-commerce in trade agreements play a crucial role in protecting digital content creators and facilitating online transactions (Gupta et al., 2021). Furthermore, harmonizing regulatory standards and reducing trade barriers can enhance market access for digital startups and SMEs, fostering a more inclusive and competitive digital ecosystem (Chen & Mattoo, 2018).

However, negotiating digital trade agreements poses several challenges, ranging from differing national regulatory frameworks to concerns about digital sovereignty and cybersecurity (Lee, 2020). Moreover, the rapid pace of technological advancement often outpaces the capacity of policymakers to formulate effective regulatory responses, creating regulatory gaps and uncertainties (Smith, 2020). Thus, digital trade agreements must strike a delicate balance between promoting innovation and ensuring regulatory coherence to maximize their economic benefits.

In conclusion, digital trade and economic agreements play a pivotal role in shaping the global digital economy, facilitating cross-border transactions, and driving innovation. By addressing regulatory barriers and promoting interoperability, these agreements can unlock the full potential of digital trade while safeguarding consumer interests and data privacy. However, policymakers must remain vigilant in addressing emerging challenges and adapting regulatory frameworks to keep pace with the evolving digital landscape.

9.3 Fostering Innovation and Entrepreneurship in Digital Economies

In the rapidly evolving landscape of digital economies, fostering innovation and entrepreneurship is essential for driving sustainable economic growth and competitiveness. As digital technologies continue to disrupt traditional industries and create new opportunities, policymakers face the challenge of creating an enabling environment that supports the emergence of innovative startups and facilitates their growth. According to Schumpeter (1934), entrepreneurship serves as the engine of economic progress, driving innovation, productivity gains, and job creation.

To nurture innovation and entrepreneurship in digital economies, policymakers must adopt a multifaceted approach that addresses various dimensions of the entrepreneurial ecosystem. This includes creating conducive regulatory frameworks that promote competition, protect intellectual property rights, and facilitate access to finance (Acs & Audretsch, 2010). Additionally, investing in digital infrastructure and promoting digital literacy are crucial for equipping entrepreneurs with the tools and skills needed to leverage digital technologies effectively (OECD, 2018).

Government support programs, such as incubators, accelerators, and innovation hubs, play a vital role in nurturing entrepreneurial talent and fostering collaboration between startups, corporates, and research institutions (Isenberg, 2010). Moreover, fostering a culture of risk-taking and experimentation is essential for encouraging entrepreneurship in digital economies (Florida, 2002). By embracing failure as an inherent part of the innovation process, entrepreneurs can learn from setbacks and iterate on their ideas more effectively.

However, fostering innovation and entrepreneurship in digital economies also entails addressing a range of challenges, including regulatory barriers, access to financing, and talent shortages (Chesbrough, 2003). In particular, regulatory uncertainty and outdated laws can stifle innovation and deter investment in emerging technologies (Cohen & Winn, 2007). Therefore, policymakers must engage in continuous dialogue with industry stakeholders to identify regulatory bottlenecks and implement agile regulatory frameworks that foster innovation while addressing legitimate concerns related to consumer protection and privacy (Sussan & Acs, 2017).

In conclusion, fostering innovation and entrepreneurship in digital economies is essential for driving economic growth, job creation, and societal progress. By adopting a holistic approach that combines supportive policies, investments in digital infrastructure, and a culture of entrepreneurship, policymakers can create an enabling environment that empowers entrepreneurs to harness the transformative potential of digital technologies.

9.3. Addressing Economic Challenges and Opportunities through Digital Diplomacy

In an increasingly interconnected world, digital diplomacy has emerged as a powerful tool for addressing economic challenges and seizing opportunities in the global arena. As nations navigate the complexities of the digital economy, leveraging digital diplomacy allows them to forge strategic partnerships, promote economic cooperation, and tackle shared challenges. Digital diplomacy refers to the use of digital technologies, including social media, data analytics, and online platforms, to advance diplomatic objectives and engage with international stakeholders (Hocking & Melissen, 2015).

One of the primary objectives of digital diplomacy in the economic realm is to facilitate trade and investment by reducing barriers and enhancing market access. Through digital channels, diplomats can engage with foreign counterparts, negotiate trade agreements, and promote their country's economic interests (Kurbalija, 2018). Digital platforms also offer opportunities for businesses to showcase their products and services to a global audience, fostering cross-border trade and investment flows (Carpenter, 2016).

Furthermore, digital diplomacy plays a crucial role in addressing emerging economic challenges, such as cybersecurity threats and digital protectionism. By fostering international cooperation and information sharing, diplomats can work together to develop norms and regulations that promote a secure and open digital environment (Ferreira-Pereira & Tavares, 2020). Additionally, digital diplomacy can help mitigate the risks of trade conflicts and economic sanctions by facilitating dialogue and negotiation between countries (Rana, 2019).

However, digital diplomacy also poses its own set of challenges, including issues related to digital divide, privacy concerns, and information manipulation (Bjola & Pamment, 2018). Not all countries have equal access to digital technologies, which can exacerbate existing economic inequalities and hinder participation in the global digital economy (Nye, 2017). Moreover, the proliferation of disinformation and fake news on digital platforms can undermine trust and diplomatic efforts, complicating international relations (Rosenberger & Winkler, 2020).

In conclusion, digital diplomacy offers unprecedented opportunities for addressing economic challenges and fostering cooperation in the digital age. By leveraging digital technologies effectively, diplomats can promote trade, investment, and economic development while navigating complex geopolitical dynamics. However, to realize the full potential of digital diplomacy, it is essential to address the underlying issues of digital divide, privacy, and misinformation, ensuring that all countries can benefit from the opportunities offered by the digital economy.

10. Environmental Diplomacy in the Digital Age

"Digital tools offer new avenues for enhancing transparency, monitoring environmental impacts, and engaging stakeholders in diplomatic efforts to protect the planet." - Mary Robinson

In the face of escalating environmental challenges, diplomacy has become increasingly crucial for fostering international cooperation and collective action to address issues such as climate change, biodiversity loss, and pollution. With the advent of the digital age, environmental diplomacy has undergone a transformative shift, offering new opportunities for collaboration, information sharing, and public engagement (Hurrell & Kingsbury, 2013).

Digital technologies have revolutionized the way environmental diplomacy is conducted, enabling real-time communication, data sharing, and collaborative problem-solving on a global scale. For instance, online platforms and social media channels provide diplomats with tools to engage with stakeholders, raise awareness about environmental issues, and mobilize support for sustainable solutions (Falkner, 2016). Moreover, digital mapping technologies and remote sensing allow policymakers to monitor environmental changes and assess their impact more accurately (Haddad, 2019).

One of the key advantages of digital diplomacy in the environmental realm is its ability to facilitate multistakeholder collaboration and information exchange. By leveraging digital platforms, diplomats can convene virtual meetings, workshops, and conferences that bring together government officials, scientists, NGOs, and other stakeholders to share knowledge, best practices, and resources (Vandeveer & Selin, 2018). This inclusive approach fosters a sense of ownership and collective responsibility, enhancing the effectiveness of environmental diplomacy efforts (Biermann & Gupta, 2011).

Furthermore, digital diplomacy can play a pivotal role in advancing global environmental governance by enhancing transparency, accountability, and public participation. Through open data initiatives and citizen science projects, governments can harness the collective intelligence of citizens to monitor environmental conditions, track illegal activities, and advocate for policy changes (Bulkeley & Betsill, 2005). Additionally, digital platforms enable greater transparency in international negotiations, allowing civil society organizations and the public to scrutinize decision-making processes and hold governments accountable for their commitments (Harrison & Sundstrom, 2019).

However, digital diplomacy in environmental governance also poses challenges, including issues related to data privacy, cybersecurity, and digital divide (Zwitter, 2019). Not all countries have equal access to digital technologies, which can exacerbate existing inequalities and limit participation in global environmental initiatives (O'Neill & Smith, 2014). Moreover, the proliferation of disinformation and misinformation on digital platforms can undermine trust and hinder diplomatic efforts to address environmental challenges (Gleick, 2010).

Environmental diplomacy in the digital age holds immense potential for advancing global sustainability goals and addressing pressing environmental challenges. By leveraging digital technologies effectively, diplomats can foster collaboration, transparency, and public engagement, leading to more informed decision-making and meaningful action on environmental issues. However, to realize the full benefits of digital diplomacy, it is essential to address the underlying issues of digital divide, privacy, and misinformation, ensuring that all countries can participate equitably in global environmental governance.

10.1 Leveraging Digital Tools for Environmental Diplomacy

In the quest for global environmental sustainability, the use of digital tools has emerged as a powerful strategy for enhancing the effectiveness of environmental diplomacy. By leveraging digital technologies, diplomats and environmental advocates can facilitate collaboration, data sharing, and public engagement on a scale never before possible (Kamieniecki & Kroll-Smith, 2018).

One of the primary ways digital tools enhance environmental diplomacy is through improved communication and collaboration among stakeholders. Platforms such as virtual meeting software, online forums, and social media networks enable diplomats, scientists, policymakers, and civil society representatives to exchange information, share best practices, and coordinate efforts in real time (Falkner, 2016). This fosters a sense of collective ownership and facilitates the development of innovative solutions to complex environmental challenges (Selin & VanDeveer, 2015).

Moreover, digital tools offer unprecedented opportunities for data collection, analysis, and visualization, empowering decision-makers with valuable insights into environmental trends and dynamics (Haddad, 2019). Geographic information systems (GIS), remote sensing technologies, and big data analytics enable diplomats to monitor environmental changes, assess their impact, and identify areas in need of intervention (Burch & Sheppard, 2017). This data-driven approach enhances the evidence base for policy-making and strengthens the credibility of environmental diplomacy initiatives (Lechner, 2020).

Digital tools also play a crucial role in engaging the public and raising awareness about environmental issues. Through social media campaigns, online petitions, and interactive websites, diplomats can mobilize public support for environmental initiatives and amplify the voices of affected communities (Harrison & Sundstrom, 2019). By fostering a sense of global citizenship and solidarity, digital diplomacy empowers individuals to take action and hold governments accountable for their environmental commitments (Bulkeley & Betsill, 2005).

However, leveraging digital tools for environmental diplomacy also presents challenges, including issues related to data privacy, cybersecurity, and digital literacy (Zwitter, 2019). Diplomats must navigate these complexities carefully to ensure the responsible use of digital technologies and mitigate potential risks (Falkner, 2016). Moreover, disparities in access to digital infrastructure and technology can exacerbate inequalities and limit the participation of marginalized communities in environmental decision-making processes (O'Neill & Smith, 2014).

In conclusion, digital tools offer immense potential for enhancing the impact of environmental diplomacy and advancing global sustainability goals. By facilitating collaboration, data-driven decision-making, and public engagement, digital diplomacy enables diplomats to address environmental challenges more effectively and mobilize support for meaningful action. However, to realize the full benefits of digital diplomacy, it is essential to address the underlying issues of digital divide, privacy, and cybersecurity, ensuring that all stakeholders can participate equitably in environmental governance efforts.

10.2 Collaborative Efforts in Climate Change Mitigation and Adaptation

Climate change presents one of the most pressing challenges of our time, demanding coordinated and collaborative efforts at both local and global levels to mitigate its impacts and adapt to its consequences. By fostering partnerships and cooperation among governments, civil society, businesses, and communities, collaborative efforts can enhance resilience, accelerate progress, and catalyze innovative solutions in the face of climate change (Betsill & Bulkeley, 2007).

One of the key principles underpinning collaborative efforts in climate change mitigation and adaptation is the recognition of shared responsibility and common but differentiated responsibilities (CBDR). Developed countries, historically the largest contributors to greenhouse gas emissions, have a moral obligation to take the lead in reducing emissions and providing support to vulnerable countries for adaptation (Levin, Cashore, Bernstein, & Auld, 2012). Collaborative initiatives such as the Paris Agreement provide a framework for collective action, setting targets and commitments to limit global warming and enhance resilience to climate impacts (UNFCCC, 2015).

Moreover, collaborative efforts in climate change mitigation and adaptation leverage the expertise, resources, and knowledge of diverse stakeholders to address complex challenges. Public-private partnerships, for example, enable businesses to contribute financial resources, technical expertise, and innovative technologies to climate action initiatives (Hoffman, 2017). Similarly, collaboration between scientists, policymakers, and local communities facilitates the co-design and implementation of adaptation strategies that are contextually relevant and socially equitable (Adger et al., 2009).

Furthermore, collaborative approaches to climate change mitigation and adaptation promote learning, capacity-building, and knowledge exchange among stakeholders. Platforms such as the United Nations Framework Convention on Climate Change (UNFCCC) facilitate dialogue and information-sharing, enabling countries to learn from each other's experiences and best practices (Bodansky, 2016). Additionally, networks of cities, regions, and organizations, such as the C40 Cities Climate Leadership Group and the Climate Action Network, provide avenues for peer-to-peer learning and collaboration on climate action (Bulkeley, Andonova, Betsill, Compagnon, Hale, Hoffmann, Newell, & Roger, 2014).

However, collaborative efforts in climate change mitigation and adaptation also face challenges, including issues related to governance, financing, and political will (Gupta, Pahl-Wostl, Zondervan, & de Bremond, 2013). Coordinating diverse stakeholders with competing interests and priorities can be complex, requiring effective leadership, negotiation, and consensus-building (Cashore, Auld, & Newsom, 2004). Moreover, securing adequate funding for climate action remains a persistent challenge, particularly for developing countries with limited resources and capacities (Buchner et al., 2019). Political barriers, including resistance from vested interests and short-term electoral cycles, can also impede progress on collaborative climate action initiatives (Jordan, Wurzel, & Zito, 2003).

Collaborative efforts in climate change mitigation and adaptation are essential for building resilience, accelerating progress, and achieving the goals set forth in international agreements such as the Paris Agreement and the Sustainable Development Goals (SDGs). By fostering partnerships, leveraging diverse expertise, and promoting learning and knowledge exchange, collaborative approaches can unlock synergies, overcome barriers, and catalyze transformative change in the global fight against climate change.

10.3 Addressing Global Environmental Challenges through Digital Cooperation

In the face of escalating global environmental challenges, digital cooperation has emerged as a powerful mechanism for facilitating collaboration, innovation, and collective action on a planetary scale. By harnessing the transformative potential of digital technologies, stakeholders from diverse sectors and regions can work together to address pressing environmental issues such as climate change, biodiversity loss, and pollution (Biermann & Pattberg, 2012).

Digital cooperation offers a range of opportunities for addressing global environmental challenges, including enhanced data collection, analysis, and sharing. Advanced technologies such as remote sensing, geographic information systems (GIS), and big data analytics enable scientists, policymakers, and practitioners to monitor environmental changes, assess their impacts, and develop evidence-based solutions (Mayer-Schönberger & Cukier, 2013). Moreover, digital platforms facilitate the exchange of knowledge, best practices, and resources among stakeholders, fostering collaboration and accelerating progress (Kamieniecki & Kroll-Smith, 2018).

One of the key advantages of digital cooperation in addressing environmental challenges is its ability to foster inclusivity and participation. Online platforms and social media networks provide avenues for engaging a diverse range of stakeholders, including governments, civil society organizations, businesses, and communities (Haddad, 2019). By facilitating dialogue, consultation, and decision-making in virtual spaces, digital cooperation enables the voices of marginalized groups and vulnerable populations to be heard, ensuring that environmental policies and initiatives are equitable and socially just (Bulkeley & Betsill, 2005).

Furthermore, digital cooperation can catalyze innovation and creativity in the development of sustainable solutions to environmental problems. Crowdsourcing platforms, hackathons, and open innovation initiatives harness the collective intelligence and creativity of global communities to tackle complex challenges (Lechner, 2020). By tapping into the expertise and ingenuity of diverse stakeholders, digital cooperation generates novel ideas, technologies, and approaches that have the potential to transform the way we address environmental issues (Hoffman, 2017).

However, digital cooperation in addressing global environmental challenges also poses challenges and risks that must be addressed. Issues such as data privacy, cybersecurity, and digital divide require careful attention to ensure that the benefits of digital technologies are equitably distributed and that vulnerable populations are not left behind (Zwitter, 2019). Moreover, navigating the complexities of digital governance, including issues of interoperability, standardization, and regulation, requires collaborative efforts and multistakeholder engagement (Betsill & Bulkeley, 2007).

Digital cooperation offers immense potential for addressing global environmental challenges and advancing sustainability goals. By leveraging digital technologies to facilitate collaboration, innovation, and participation, stakeholders can harness the collective power of global networks to develop effective solutions to complex environmental problems. However, realizing the full potential of digital cooperation requires addressing challenges related to inclusivity, privacy, security, and governance, ensuring that digital technologies serve the interests of people and the planet.

10.4 Promoting Sustainable Development Goals via Digital Diplomatic Initiatives

In the pursuit of achieving the Sustainable Development Goals (SDGs), digital diplomatic initiatives have emerged as powerful tools for advancing global cooperation, fostering innovation, and promoting sustainable development. By harnessing the capabilities of digital technologies, diplomats can engage with diverse stakeholders, amplify their voices, and catalyze action on a range of pressing challenges, from poverty and inequality to climate change and environmental degradation (Falkner, 2016).

Digital diplomatic initiatives offer a range of opportunities for promoting the SDGs, including enhancing communication and advocacy efforts. Social media platforms, digital campaigns, and online forums enable diplomats to raise awareness about the SDGs, share success stories, and mobilize support for sustainable development initiatives (UNDP, 2020). By leveraging the reach and immediacy of digital channels, diplomats can engage with global audiences, including youth, civil society organizations, and private sector actors, to galvanize collective action (Harrison & Sundstrom, 2019).

Moreover, digital diplomatic initiatives facilitate collaboration and knowledge exchange among stakeholders, fostering partnerships for SDG implementation. Virtual conferences, webinars, and online platforms provide spaces for dialogue, networking, and capacity-building, enabling governments, NGOs, academia, and businesses to share expertise, resources, and best practices (Haddad, 2019). By promoting cross-sectoral collaboration and South-South cooperation, digital diplomacy accelerates progress towards the achievement of the SDGs (Bulkeley & Betsill, 2005).

Furthermore, digital technologies enable diplomats to collect, analyze, and visualize data to inform policy-making and monitor progress on the SDGs. Big data analytics, geographic information systems (GIS), and remote sensing technologies provide insights into development trends, identify areas of intervention, and track the impact of interventions over time (Mayer-Schönberger & Cukier, 2013). By harnessing the power of data-driven diplomacy, policymakers can make evidence-based decisions and allocate resources more effectively to address the root causes of poverty, inequality, and environmental degradation (Betsill & Bulkeley, 2007).

However, promoting the SDGs via digital diplomatic initiatives also poses challenges that must be addressed. Issues such as digital divide, data privacy, and cybersecurity require attention to ensure that the benefits of digital technologies are equitably distributed and that vulnerable populations are not left behind (Zwitter, 2019). Moreover, navigating the complexities of digital governance, including issues of interoperability, standardization, and regulation, requires collaboration and coordination among governments, international organizations, and other stakeholders (Hoffman, 2017).

Digital diplomatic initiatives offer significant opportunities for promoting the SDGs and advancing sustainable development globally. By leveraging digital technologies to enhance communication, collaboration, and data-driven decision-making, diplomats can mobilize support, build partnerships, and drive progress towards the achievement of the SDGs. However, realizing the full potential of digital diplomacy requires addressing challenges related to inclusivity, privacy, security, and governance, ensuring that digital technologies serve the interests of people and the planet.

11. Gender Diplomacy: Empowering Women in the Digital Sphere

"Gender-responsive diplomacy in the digital realm requires concerted efforts to challenge stereotypes, promote digital skills training, and create enabling environments for women's leadership and innovation." - Phoebe Schreiner

Gender diplomacy in the digital sphere is an essential component of efforts to promote gender equality, empower women, and advance inclusive development globally. As digital technologies continue to reshape the way we communicate, work, and interact, it is crucial to ensure that women have equal access to and participation in the digital economy (Htun & Weldon, 2012).

One of the key aspects of gender diplomacy in the digital sphere is addressing the digital gender gap, which refers to disparities in access to and use of digital technologies between men and women (ITU, 2019). Digital inclusion initiatives, such as training programs, mentorship schemes, and technology literacy campaigns, are essential for equipping women with the skills and confidence to navigate the digital world and leverage its opportunities (UN Women, 2020). By bridging the digital gender gap, gender diplomats can unlock the potential of women as drivers of innovation, entrepreneurship, and economic growth (Huyer, 2016).

Moreover, gender diplomacy in the digital sphere involves advocating for policies and regulations that promote women's rights and ensure their safety and security online (Gurumurthy et al., 2012). This includes combating online harassment and violence against women, protecting privacy and data rights, and promoting digital literacy and digital rights education (UNESCO, 2019). By advocating for a safe and inclusive digital environment, gender diplomats can create enabling conditions for women to fully participate in digital society and exercise their rights (MacKinnon, 2012).

Furthermore, gender diplomacy in the digital sphere entails leveraging digital technologies to amplify women's voices, experiences, and perspectives in decision-making processes (Hafkin & Huyer, 2006). Social media platforms, online forums, and digital storytelling initiatives provide spaces for women to share their stories, advocate for their rights, and mobilize support for gender equality (Powell & Geist, 2015). By harnessing the power of digital advocacy and networking, gender diplomats can advance women's rights agendas and drive social and political change (Kantarci et al., 2019).

However, gender diplomacy in the digital sphere also faces challenges and risks that must be addressed. These include online gender-based violence, digital literacy gaps, and cultural barriers to women's participation in digital spaces (UNICEF, 2020). Moreover, the digital divide between urban and rural areas, as well as between developed and developing countries, exacerbates inequalities and limits opportunities for women's empowerment (World Bank, 2019). Gender diplomats must work collaboratively with governments, civil society, and technology companies to overcome these challenges and create an inclusive digital future for all.

Gender diplomacy in the digital sphere is essential for promoting women's rights, empowering women, and advancing gender equality in the digital age. By bridging the digital gender gap, advocating for women's digital rights, and amplifying women's voices online, gender diplomats can contribute to building a more inclusive and equitable digital society. However, addressing the challenges and risks associated with gender diplomacy in the digital sphere requires concerted efforts and collaboration across sectors and stakeholders.

11.1 Promoting Gender Equality through Digital Diplomacy

Gender equality is not only a fundamental human right but also a key driver of sustainable development, economic growth, and peace. Digital diplomacy, the use of digital technologies in diplomatic efforts, presents unique opportunities for promoting gender equality on a global scale by leveraging the power of technology to amplify women's voices, advance women's rights, and foster inclusive development (Htun & Weldon, 2012).

One of the primary ways digital diplomacy promotes gender equality is by amplifying women's voices and experiences in digital spaces. Social media platforms, online forums, and digital storytelling initiatives provide women with platforms to share their stories, advocate for their rights, and connect with global networks of support (Powell & Geist, 2015). By elevating women's voices and highlighting their perspectives, digital diplomacy challenges gender stereotypes and fosters greater recognition of women's contributions to society (MacKinnon, 2012).

Moreover, digital diplomacy enables governments, international organizations, and civil society actors to collaborate and coordinate efforts to advance gender equality agendas. Virtual meetings, webinars, and online platforms facilitate dialogue, knowledge-sharing, and capacity-building among stakeholders, enabling them to exchange best practices, mobilize resources, and develop innovative solutions to address gender disparities (UN Women, 2020). By fostering cross-sectoral collaboration and South-South cooperation, digital diplomacy accelerates progress towards achieving gender equality targets (Bulkeley & Betsill, 2005).

Furthermore, digital diplomacy plays a crucial role in advocating for policies and regulations that promote gender equality and protect women's rights in digital spaces. Diplomatic efforts can focus on combating online harassment and violence against women, ensuring equal access to digital technologies and digital literacy programs, and promoting women's leadership and participation in decision-making processes related to technology and innovation (Gurumurthy et al., 2012). By advocating for a safe, inclusive, and gender-responsive digital environment, digital diplomats can create enabling conditions for women to fully participate in the digital economy and society (Hafkin & Huyer, 2006).

However, promoting gender equality through digital diplomacy also faces challenges and risks that must be addressed. These include digital divides related to access to technology and digital literacy, online gender-based violence, and data privacy and security concerns (UNICEF, 2020). Moreover, cultural and social norms that perpetuate gender stereotypes and discrimination may pose barriers to women's participation in digital diplomacy initiatives (World Bank, 2019). Digital diplomats must work collaboratively with governments, civil society, and technology companies to overcome these challenges and ensure that digital technologies contribute to, rather than exacerbate, gender inequalities.

In conclusion, digital diplomacy has the potential to be a powerful tool for promoting gender equality and advancing women's rights in the digital age. By amplifying women's voices, fostering collaboration among stakeholders, and advocating for gender-responsive policies and regulations, digital diplomats can contribute to creating a more inclusive and equitable world for all. However, addressing the challenges and risks associated with promoting gender equality through digital diplomacy requires concerted efforts and collaboration across sectors and stakeholders.

11.2 Amplifying Women's Voices in Online Spaces

Amplifying women's voices in online spaces is crucial for promoting gender equality, challenging stereotypes, and fostering diverse perspectives in digital discourse. As the digital landscape continues to evolve, it is essential to ensure that women have equal opportunities to participate, contribute, and lead in online conversations (Powell & Geist-Martin, 2015).

One effective strategy for amplifying women's voices in online spaces is to create inclusive digital environments that prioritize diversity, equity, and inclusion. This involves establishing clear guidelines and community standards that prohibit harassment, discrimination, and hate speech, and fostering a culture of respect, empathy, and support (UN Women, 2020). By creating safe and welcoming spaces, online platforms can encourage women to share their ideas, experiences, and perspectives without fear of backlash or retaliation.

Moreover, digital platforms can implement features and tools that amplify women's voices and promote their visibility. For example, algorithms can be designed to prioritize content created by women and to surface diverse voices in search results and recommendations (Gürsel & Son, 2019). Additionally, online communities can feature women-led initiatives, campaigns, and discussions prominently to highlight their contributions and achievements (Harrison & Sundstrom, 2019). By leveraging technology to amplify women's voices, digital platforms can counteract biases and inequalities that exist in offline spaces.

Furthermore, online spaces can facilitate opportunities for women to connect, collaborate, and support each other through networks, forums, and virtual communities. Women-focused online groups, mentorship programs, and peer support networks provide avenues for women to share resources, seek advice, and build solidarity (Hafkin & Huyer, 2006). Additionally, online events, webinars, and conferences can bring together women from diverse backgrounds and fields to exchange ideas, build networks, and amplify their collective voice (Bates et al., 2003). By fostering connections and collaborations among women, online spaces can strengthen their influence and impact in digital discourse.

However, amplifying women's voices in online spaces also requires addressing barriers and challenges that prevent women from fully participating and engaging. These include online harassment, cyberbullying, and trolling, which disproportionately target women and discourage them from speaking out (UNICEF, 2020). Additionally, digital divides related to access to technology, digital literacy, and connectivity limit women's ability to participate in online conversations, particularly in low-income and marginalized communities (World Bank, 2019). Addressing these barriers requires comprehensive efforts to promote digital inclusion, combat online harassment, and bridge digital divides to ensure that all women can participate and thrive in online spaces.

Amplifying women's voices in online spaces is essential for creating inclusive digital environments, challenging stereotypes, and advancing gender equality. By creating safe and welcoming spaces, leveraging technology to promote visibility, and facilitating connections and collaborations among women, online platforms can empower women to share their perspectives, contribute to digital discourse, and shape the future of the internet. However, addressing barriers and challenges to women's participation requires concerted efforts from governments, civil society, and technology companies to ensure that online spaces are truly inclusive and equitable for all.

11.3 Engaging Men and Boys as Allies in Gender Diplomacy Efforts

Engaging men and boys as allies in gender diplomacy efforts is essential for advancing gender equality and fostering inclusive societies. By involving men and boys as partners in the pursuit of gender justice, diplomatic initiatives can challenge harmful gender norms, promote positive masculinity, and create transformative change (Kaufman, 2017).

One effective strategy for engaging men and boys as allies in gender diplomacy efforts is to promote awareness and education about gender equality and its benefits for all genders. Diplomatic initiatives can develop educational programs, campaigns, and workshops that target men and boys, providing them with opportunities to learn about gender inequality, its root causes, and its impact on individuals and communities (Connell, 2019). By raising awareness and promoting dialogue, diplomatic efforts can foster empathy, understanding, and solidarity among men and boys, motivating them to become advocates for gender equality.

Moreover, gender diplomacy efforts can involve men and boys as active participants in the design, implementation, and evaluation of gender equality policies and programs. By engaging men and boys in decision-making processes, diplomatic initiatives can ensure that their perspectives, experiences, and needs are taken into account (Flood & Pease, 2009). This may involve creating platforms for men's groups, fathers' networks, and male allies to collaborate with governments, civil society organizations, and women's rights advocates on gender equality initiatives (Barker et al., 2011). By involving men and boys as partners, gender diplomacy efforts can generate greater buy-in, ownership, and sustainability.

Furthermore, gender diplomacy efforts can work to transform harmful gender norms and stereotypes that perpetuate inequality and discrimination. Diplomatic initiatives can develop targeted campaigns and interventions that challenge traditional notions of masculinity and promote alternative models of manhood that are based on respect, equality, and non-violence (Jewkes & Flood, 2014). This may involve engaging with cultural and religious leaders, media professionals, and influencers to promote positive representations of men and boys and to challenge harmful portrayals of gender in the media and popular culture (Pettman, 2017). By promoting positive masculinity, gender diplomacy efforts can create enabling environments for men and boys to support gender equality and challenge sexism and misogyny.

However, engaging men and boys as allies in gender diplomacy efforts also requires addressing resistance, backlash, and power dynamics that may undermine progress towards gender equality. Diplomatic initiatives must be sensitive to the ways in which privilege, patriarchy, and inequality shape men's and boys' attitudes and behaviors (Hearn & Hall,

2016). This may involve working with men's groups and organizations to address issues such as male privilege, accountability, and allyship, and to promote allyship as a collective responsibility (Kimmel, 2013). By fostering critical reflection and accountability, gender diplomacy efforts can create spaces for men and boys to confront their own biases and privilege and to commit to meaningful action for gender equality.

In conclusion, engaging men and boys as allies in gender diplomacy efforts is critical for advancing gender equality and creating inclusive societies. By promoting awareness and education, involving men and boys as partners, and challenging harmful gender norms, diplomatic initiatives can empower men and boys to become advocates for gender equality and agents of change in their communities and beyond. However, addressing resistance and power dynamics requires sustained commitment and collaboration from governments, civil society organizations, and other stakeholders to ensure that gender diplomacy efforts are truly inclusive and transformative.

12. Health Diplomacy in the Digital Era

"Digital health diplomacy holds immense potential for strengthening health systems, enhancing disease surveillance, and promoting universal access to healthcare services." - Tedros Adhanom Ghebreyesus

Health diplomacy in the digital era represents a transformative approach to addressing global health challenges by harnessing the power of technology, data, and collaboration. As the world becomes increasingly interconnected through digital channels, health diplomacy has evolved to leverage digital tools and platforms to promote cooperation, coordination, and innovation in addressing health issues at the global level (Kickbusch et al., 2016).

One of the key aspects of health diplomacy in the digital era is the use of digital technologies to facilitate information sharing, communication, and coordination among countries, organizations, and stakeholders involved in health governance. Digital platforms, such as online databases, social media networks, and virtual conferencing tools, enable real-time sharing of health data, research findings, and best practices, facilitating rapid responses to health emergencies and enabling evidence-based decision-making (Novillo-Ortiz et al., 2015). By promoting transparency and collaboration, digital health diplomacy strengthens trust and cooperation among nations and fosters collective action to address common health challenges.

Moreover, digital health diplomacy plays a crucial role in enhancing disease surveillance, monitoring, and early warning systems to detect and respond to emerging health threats. Advanced technologies, such as artificial intelligence, machine learning, and big data analytics, enable the analysis of vast amounts of health data from diverse sources, including social media, mobile phone networks, and wearable devices, to identify disease outbreaks, track the spread of infectious diseases, and assess health trends in real-time (Kaplan et al., 2020). By leveraging predictive analytics and modeling, digital health diplomacy enhances preparedness and response capabilities, enabling countries to mitigate the impact of health crises and save lives.

Furthermore, digital health diplomacy promotes capacity-building and knowledge exchange to strengthen health systems and improve health outcomes globally. Online training programs, webinars, and e-learning platforms provide opportunities for healthcare professionals, policymakers, and researchers to enhance their skills, share experiences, and learn from global best practices in areas such as pandemic preparedness, vaccine distribution, and healthcare delivery (Wang et al., 2020). By facilitating cross-border collaboration and learning, digital health diplomacy fosters innovation and adaptation, driving improvements in health services and outcomes.

However, digital health diplomacy also faces challenges and risks that must be addressed to maximize its potential impact. Issues such as data privacy, cybersecurity, and digital divide pose barriers to effective digital health cooperation, particularly in low-resource settings and marginalized communities (Agarwal et al., 2020). Moreover, ensuring the quality and reliability of health information shared through digital channels is essential to prevent misinformation and promote evidence-based decision-making (Liu et al., 2016). Digital health diplomacy requires robust governance frameworks, international standards, and ethical guidelines to safeguard the integrity, security, and inclusivity of digital health initiatives.

In conclusion, health diplomacy in the digital era offers unprecedented opportunities to advance global health cooperation and improve health outcomes worldwide. By leveraging technology to facilitate information sharing, enhance surveillance capabilities, and promote capacity-building, digital health diplomacy strengthens collaboration among nations and stakeholders, enabling more effective responses to health challenges. However, addressing challenges related to data governance, cybersecurity, and equity is essential to ensure that digital health diplomacy benefits all populations and contributes to achieving the goal of health for all.

12.1 Utilizing Digital Health Technologies for Diplomatic Purposes

Utilizing digital health technologies for diplomatic purposes represents a strategic approach to advancing global health diplomacy in the digital age, leveraging technology to strengthen cooperation, collaboration, and innovation in addressing health challenges worldwide. Digital health technologies offer unprecedented opportunities to enhance diplomatic efforts in promoting health, preventing disease, and achieving equitable access to healthcare services (Kaplan et al., 2020).

One of the key ways digital health technologies can be utilized for diplomatic purposes is through promoting information sharing and transparency among nations and stakeholders. Digital platforms, such as online databases, health information systems, and mobile applications, enable real-time sharing of health data, research findings, and best practices, facilitating evidence-based decision-making and policy formulation (Novillo-Ortiz et al., 2015). By fostering open communication and collaboration, digital health technologies strengthen trust and cooperation among countries, paving the way for joint efforts to address global health challenges.

Moreover, digital health technologies play a crucial role in enhancing disease surveillance, monitoring, and response capabilities to address emerging health threats. Advanced technologies, including artificial intelligence, machine learning, and big data analytics, enable the analysis of vast amounts of health data from diverse sources to detect disease outbreaks, track the spread of infectious diseases, and predict health trends (Kaplan et al., 2020). By leveraging predictive analytics and modeling, digital health technologies empower diplomats and policymakers to anticipate and respond proactively to health crises, minimizing their impact on populations.

Furthermore, digital health technologies facilitate capacity-building and knowledge exchange to strengthen health systems and improve health outcomes globally. Online training programs, webinars, and e-learning platforms provide opportunities for healthcare professionals, policymakers, and researchers to enhance their skills, share experiences, and learn from global best practices in areas such as disease management, health promotion, and healthcare delivery (Wang et al., 2020). By promoting cross-border collaboration and learning, digital health technologies drive innovation and adaptation, fostering sustainable improvements in health services and outcomes.

Additionally, digital health technologies can be utilized for diplomatic purposes in promoting public health diplomacy initiatives and campaigns. Digital platforms, such as social media networks, online forums, and mobile applications, provide channels for engaging with diverse audiences, raising awareness about health issues, and mobilizing support for health-related initiatives (Harrison & Sundstrom, 2019). By harnessing the power of digital advocacy and communication, diplomats can amplify their messages, reach broader audiences, and foster public engagement and participation in health promotion efforts.

However, utilizing digital health technologies for diplomatic purposes also presents challenges and risks that must be addressed to maximize their potential impact. Issues such as data privacy, cybersecurity, and digital divide pose barriers to effective digital health cooperation, particularly in low-resource settings and marginalized communities (Agarwal et al., 2020). Moreover, ensuring the quality and reliability of health information shared through digital channels is essential to prevent misinformation and promote evidence-based decision-making (Liu et al., 2016). Digital health diplomacy requires robust governance frameworks, international standards, and ethical guidelines to safeguard the integrity, security, and inclusivity of digital health initiatives.

Utilizing digital health technologies for diplomatic purposes offers unprecedented opportunities to advance global health diplomacy and improve health outcomes worldwide. By promoting information sharing, enhancing disease surveillance, facilitating capacity-building, and engaging in public health diplomacy initiatives, diplomats can leverage technology to strengthen cooperation, collaboration, and innovation in addressing health challenges. However, addressing challenges related to data governance, cybersecurity, and equity is essential to ensure that digital health diplomacy benefits all populations and contributes to achieving the goal of health for all.

12.2 Collaborative Efforts in Global Health Security and Pandemic Preparedness

Collaborative efforts in global health security and pandemic preparedness are essential for strengthening resilience and mitigating the impact of health emergencies on a global scale. By fostering cooperation, coordination, and solidarity among nations, international organizations, and stakeholders, collaborative initiatives enhance preparedness, response, and recovery capabilities, reducing the risks posed by infectious disease outbreaks and other health threats (Heymann et al., 2015).

One of the key aspects of collaborative efforts in global health security is the establishment of multilateral frameworks and partnerships to facilitate information sharing, joint planning, and resource mobilization. Initiatives such as the Global Health Security Agenda (GHSA) bring together governments, international organizations, and civil society to strengthen health systems, enhance surveillance capabilities, and improve preparedness for public health emergencies (Katz et al., 2017). By promoting collaboration and coordination across borders, multilateral frameworks enable countries to pool their expertise, resources, and experiences to address common health challenges.

Moreover, collaborative efforts in global health security involve capacity-building and technical assistance to strengthen health systems and build resilience at the national and regional levels. International organizations, such as the World Health Organization (WHO) and the Centers for

Disease Control and Prevention (CDC), provide training, technical support, and guidance to countries in areas such as disease surveillance, laboratory diagnostics, and outbreak response (Mackenzie et al., 2018). By building local capacities and empowering frontline healthcare workers, collaborative initiatives enhance the ability of countries to detect, respond to, and contain health threats.

Furthermore, collaborative efforts in global health security emphasize the importance of data sharing, research collaboration, and innovation to improve preparedness and response capabilities. International networks, such as the Global Outbreak Alert and Response Network (GOARN) and the Coalition for Epidemic Preparedness Innovations (CEPI), facilitate rapid sharing of scientific data, research findings, and best practices during health emergencies (Gostin et al., 2014). By promoting open science and collaboration, these networks accelerate the development of vaccines, therapeutics, and diagnostics, enabling faster and more effective responses to emerging health threats.

Additionally, collaborative efforts in global health security involve promoting community engagement, risk communication, and public trust to enhance resilience and response capabilities. Effective risk communication strategies, including transparent, timely, and accurate information sharing, help build public confidence, reduce panic, and facilitate compliance with public health measures during health emergencies (World Health Organization, 2020). By engaging communities, empowering local leaders, and addressing cultural and social factors, collaborative initiatives strengthen community resilience and enhance the effectiveness of public health interventions.

However, collaborative efforts in global health security also face challenges and barriers that must be addressed to maximize their impact. These include political tensions, resource constraints, and competing priorities that may undermine cooperation and solidarity among nations (Fidler, 2016). Moreover, addressing structural inequalities, including disparities in access to healthcare and essential services, is essential to ensure that collaborative efforts are equitable and inclusive (Gates et al., 2020). Collaborative initiatives must also navigate ethical and governance challenges related to data sharing, privacy protection, and intellectual property rights to ensure that the benefits of research and innovation are shared equitably.

Collaborative efforts in global health security and pandemic preparedness are essential for strengthening resilience and mitigating the impact of health emergencies on a global scale. By fostering cooperation, coordination, and solidarity among nations and stakeholders, collaborative initiatives enhance preparedness, response, and recovery capabilities, reducing the risks posed by infectious disease outbreaks and other health threats. However, addressing challenges related to political tensions, resource constraints, and structural inequalities requires sustained commitment and collaboration from governments, international organizations, and civil society to ensure that collaborative efforts are effective, equitable, and inclusive.

12.3 Addressing Health Inequities through Digital Diplomatic Initiatives

Addressing health inequities through digital diplomatic initiatives is a strategic approach to promoting equity, access, and inclusion in healthcare delivery and outcomes. By harnessing the power of technology and diplomacy, these initiatives aim to bridge gaps in healthcare access, reduce disparities, and improve health outcomes for marginalized populations globally (Liu et al., 2021).

One of the primary ways digital diplomatic initiatives address health inequities is by leveraging digital technologies to expand access to healthcare services and information in underserved communities. Telemedicine, mobile health (mHealth) applications, and online health platforms enable remote consultations, health education, and preventive care delivery, overcoming geographical barriers and increasing healthcare access for populations in rural and remote areas (Afrin et al., 2020). By providing virtual healthcare services, digital diplomatic initiatives ensure that marginalized populations, including those living in low-resource settings, have equitable access to quality healthcare.

Moreover, digital diplomatic initiatives promote cross-sectoral collaboration and partnerships to address the social determinants of health and tackle underlying factors contributing to health inequities. By bringing together governments, civil society organizations, private sector partners, and communities, these initiatives develop comprehensive strategies and interventions that address issues such as poverty, education, housing, and environmental conditions, which significantly impact health outcomes (World Health Organization, 2021). Through joint efforts and coordinated action, digital diplomatic initiatives foster synergies and maximize impact in addressing health disparities and promoting health equity.

Furthermore, digital diplomatic initiatives employ data-driven approaches and digital tools to identify, monitor, and address health inequities at the population level. Health information systems, electronic health records, and data analytics enable policymakers and healthcare providers to disaggregate health data by demographic factors such as age, gender, ethnicity, and socioeconomic status, allowing for targeted interventions and tailored healthcare delivery (Chang et al., 2021). By harnessing the power of data and technology, digital diplomatic initiatives facilitate evidence-based decision-making and resource allocation to address the root causes of health inequities.

Additionally, digital diplomatic initiatives engage in advocacy, awareness-raising, and capacity-building efforts to promote health equity and social justice on a global scale. Digital platforms, social media campaigns, and online advocacy tools amplify the voices of marginalized communities, raise awareness about health disparities, and mobilize support for policy changes and systemic reforms (Global Health Advocacy Incubator, n.d.). By empowering communities and advocating for policy reforms, digital diplomatic initiatives drive systemic changes that address structural barriers and promote health equity for all.

However, addressing health inequities through digital diplomatic initiatives also faces challenges and barriers that must be overcome to maximize impact. These include digital divides related to access to technology, internet connectivity, and digital literacy, which disproportionately affect marginalized populations (World Health Organization, 2021). Moreover, ensuring cultural sensitivity, community engagement, and meaningful participation of marginalized communities in digital health initiatives is essential to avoid reinforcing existing inequities (Lau et al., 2020). Digital diplomatic initiatives must prioritize inclusivity, equity, and cultural competency to ensure that their interventions effectively address the needs of the most vulnerable populations.

Addressing health inequities through digital diplomatic initiatives is a critical strategy for promoting equity, access, and inclusion in healthcare delivery and outcomes. By leveraging technology, data, and collaboration, these initiatives have the potential to bridge gaps in healthcare access, reduce disparities, and improve health outcomes for marginalized populations globally. However, addressing digital divides, ensuring cultural competency, and prioritizing community engagement are essential to ensure that digital diplomatic initiatives are effective, equitable, and inclusive in their approach to promoting health equity.

12.4 Promoting Public Health Education and Awareness Digitally

Promoting public health education and awareness digitally is a dynamic strategy for empowering individuals, communities, and societies to make informed decisions about their health and well-being. By leveraging digital platforms, tools, and innovative approaches, public health initiatives can reach diverse audiences, raise awareness about health issues, and foster positive behavior change (Barnett et al., 2020).

One of the primary ways digital platforms promote public health education and awareness is through the dissemination of accurate, timely, and accessible health information. Websites, mobile applications, and social media channels provide platforms for sharing evidence-based health resources, educational materials, and interactive content, reaching broad audiences with targeted messaging (Chou et al., 2020). By leveraging multimedia formats such as videos, infographics, and interactive quizzes, digital health education initiatives enhance engagement and understanding, making complex health topics more accessible and relatable to diverse populations.

Moreover, digital platforms facilitate community engagement and participatory approaches to public health education, empowering individuals to become active agents in promoting health and well-being. Online forums, virtual support groups, and social networking platforms provide spaces for sharing experiences, exchanging knowledge, and building solidarity around health issues (Cabaj & Weaver, 2016). By fostering peer support, community empowerment, and collective action, digital health education initiatives empower individuals to take ownership of their health and advocate for positive change in their communities.

Furthermore, digital platforms enable targeted and personalized health education interventions that address the unique needs and preferences of different populations. Data analytics, machine learning, and artificial intelligence algorithms allow for the customization of health messages, recommendations, and interventions based on individual characteristics, behaviors, and preferences (Kontos et al., 2014). By tailoring content and delivery methods to specific demographics, cultural backgrounds, and health literacy levels, digital health education initiatives enhance relevance, resonance, and effectiveness, leading to greater impact on behavior change and health outcomes.

Additionally, digital platforms play a crucial role in promoting public health education and awareness during health emergencies and crises, such as the COVID-19 pandemic. Rapid dissemination of accurate information, updates on preventive measures, and guidance on health protocols through websites, mobile apps, and social media channels help counter misinformation, reduce panic, and promote adherence to public health guidelines (Freeman et al., 2020). By providing reliable sources of information and fostering community resilience, digital health education initiatives contribute to effective pandemic response and mitigation efforts.

However, promoting public health education and awareness digitally also presents challenges and considerations that must be addressed to maximize impact and reach. These include issues related to digital literacy, access to technology, and health disparities that may limit the effectiveness of digital health education initiatives, particularly among marginalized populations (Kreuter et al., 2000). Moreover, ensuring the accuracy, credibility, and trustworthiness of health information shared online is essential to prevent the spread of misinformation and promote evidence-based decision-making (Fu et al., 2016). Digital health education initiatives must prioritize transparency, accountability, and ethical standards to build trust and credibility with their audiences.

Promoting public health education and awareness digitally is a powerful strategy for empowering individuals, communities, and societies to make informed decisions about their health. By leveraging technology, community engagement, and personalized approaches, digital health education initiatives enhance access to information, foster behavior change, and promote positive health outcomes. However, addressing challenges related to digital literacy, access, and credibility is essential to ensure that digital health education initiatives are effective, equitable, and inclusive in their efforts to promote public health.

13. Space Diplomacy: Exploring New Frontiers in the Digital Universe

"Space diplomacy in the digital era requires strategic partnerships, transparency, and inclusive participation to ensure that the benefits of space exploration and technology are shared equitably among nations and future generations." - Michael Collins

Space diplomacy represents a paradigm shift in international relations, as nations collaborate and compete in the exploration and utilization of outer space. In the digital age, advancements in space technology and communication have transformed space diplomacy, opening new frontiers for cooperation, competition, and conflict in the digital universe.

One of the primary ways space diplomacy explores new frontiers in the digital universe is through international collaboration in space exploration and research. Digital platforms facilitate real-time communication and data sharing among space agencies, researchers, and stakeholders around the world, enabling collaborative efforts in space missions, scientific discoveries, and technological innovations (Weeden & Sampson, 2020). By leveraging digital tools and networks, space diplomacy fosters partnerships that transcend geopolitical boundaries, driving progress in space exploration and advancing scientific knowledge for the benefit of humanity.

Moreover, space diplomacy in the digital universe involves strategic partnerships and alliances to address common challenges and opportunities in space activities. International agreements, treaties, and frameworks provide the legal and regulatory framework for cooperation in space exploration, satellite operations, and space debris mitigation (Johnson-Freese, 2018). Digital communication platforms facilitate negotiation, coordination, and implementation of space agreements, ensuring transparency, compliance, and peaceful use of outer space.

Furthermore, space diplomacy explores new frontiers in the digital universe through competition and rivalry among spacefaring nations and commercial entities. The digital space race encompasses efforts to develop advanced space technologies, establish space infrastructure, and assert dominance in space domains such as satellite navigation, Earth observation, and space tourism (Logsdon, 2015). Digital communication networks enable real-time monitoring and surveillance of space activities, enhancing situational awareness and strategic decision-making in space diplomacy and security.

Additionally, space diplomacy in the digital universe addresses emerging challenges and risks in space governance, cybersecurity, and space debris management. Digital technologies enable tracking, monitoring, and mitigation of space debris, reducing the risk of collisions and space hazards (Liou & Johnson, 2016). Moreover, space cybersecurity initiatives aim to protect space assets, infrastructure, and communications from cyber threats, ensuring the safety, security, and integrity of space operations in the digital age.

However, space diplomacy in the digital universe also faces governance, ethical, and security challenges that must be addressed to ensure the responsible and sustainable use of outer space. Issues such as space debris, orbital congestion, and space traffic management require international cooperation and coordination to develop norms, standards, and best practices for space sustainability (Jakhu & Pelton, 2017). Moreover, space cybersecurity threats, including hacking, jamming, and cyber espionage, pose risks to space assets and communications systems, necessitating robust cybersecurity measures and international cooperation in space security.

Space diplomacy explores new frontiers in the digital universe by leveraging technology, collaboration, and competition in space exploration and utilization. Digital communication platforms facilitate international cooperation, strategic partnerships, and competition in space activities, driving progress in space exploration, research, and governance. However, addressing governance, security, and ethical challenges is essential to ensure the responsible and sustainable use of outer space for the benefit of present and future generations.

13.1 International Cooperation in Space Exploration and Research

International cooperation in space exploration and research represents a collaborative endeavor to unlock the mysteries of the cosmos and expand humanity's presence beyond Earth. Through partnerships among space agencies, researchers, and nations, countries pool their resources, expertise, and capabilities to achieve common goals in space exploration, scientific discovery, and technological innovation (Stares, 2019).

One of the primary drivers of international cooperation in space exploration and research is the pursuit of shared scientific objectives and missions. Collaborative projects, such as the International Space Station (ISS), bring together space agencies from multiple countries to conduct scientific experiments, technology demonstrations, and human spaceflight missions in low Earth orbit (Le Gall et al., 2018). By sharing resources and expertise, international partnerships enable scientists and researchers to conduct groundbreaking research in fields such as space medicine, materials science, and astrobiology, leading to new insights into the nature of the universe and the potential for life beyond Earth.

Moreover, international cooperation in space exploration and research fosters diplomatic and geopolitical partnerships that transcend terrestrial boundaries. Space exploration initiatives, such as joint missions to the Moon, Mars, and beyond, provide opportunities for countries to collaborate on ambitious projects that push the boundaries of human knowledge and capability (Johnson, 2017). By working together on complex and challenging missions, nations build trust, cooperation, and goodwill, fostering peaceful relations and mutual understanding in the international community.

Furthermore, international cooperation in space exploration and research promotes technology transfer and capacity-building initiatives that benefit developing countries and emerging spacefaring nations. Collaborative programs, such as satellite launches, remote sensing projects, and astronaut training programs, enable countries to access space technology, expertise, and infrastructure that they may not possess independently (Weeden & Johnson-Freese, 2017). By fostering skills development, knowledge exchange, and infrastructure investment, international partnerships empower countries to participate more actively in the global space economy and contribute to scientific advancement and innovation.

Additionally, international cooperation in space exploration and research addresses global challenges and opportunities that transcend national boundaries, such as climate change, natural disasters, and planetary defense. Collaborative efforts, such as Earth observation missions, climate monitoring satellites, and asteroid detection programs, provide critical data and information for addressing pressing environmental and planetary challenges (Fricker et al., 2020). By pooling resources and expertise, countries enhance their collective ability to address shared threats and opportunities in space and on Earth.

However, international cooperation in space exploration and research also faces challenges and barriers that must be overcome to maximize its potential impact. These include geopolitical tensions, budget constraints, and divergent national interests that may hinder collaboration and coordination among spacefaring nations (Frans von der Dunk, 2020). Moreover, ensuring equitable participation, benefit-sharing, and transparency in international space projects is essential to avoid disparities and promote inclusivity in the global space community (Hsu et al., 2017). International cooperation in space exploration and research requires sustained commitment, diplomacy, and cooperation to overcome challenges and achieve shared goals in the exploration and utilization of outer space.

In conclusion, international cooperation in space exploration and research is a testament to humanity's shared aspirations and ambitions to explore, discover, and innovate beyond Earth. By fostering collaboration, partnership, and diplomacy among spacefaring nations, countries advance scientific knowledge, promote peaceful relations, and address global challenges that transcend national boundaries. However, addressing challenges related to geopolitics, resource allocation, and inclusivity is essential to ensure that international cooperation in space exploration and research benefits all nations and contributes to the collective advancement of humanity's understanding of the cosmos.

13.2 Addressing Space Debris and Security Challenges Digitally

Addressing space debris and security challenges digitally is essential for safeguarding space assets, ensuring orbital safety, and promoting responsible space behavior in the increasingly crowded and contested space environment. By leveraging digital technologies, data analytics, and international cooperation, spacefaring nations and organizations can develop proactive strategies and solutions to mitigate the risks posed by space debris and enhance space security (Johnson-Freese, 2020).

One of the primary ways digital technologies address space debris challenges is through enhanced tracking, monitoring, and characterization of orbital debris objects. Digital sensors, ground-based radars, and space-based telescopes enable continuous surveillance of the space environment, providing real-time data on the location, trajectory, and size of debris objects (Liou & Johnson, 2016). By analyzing this data using advanced algorithms and machine learning techniques, space agencies and operators can assess collision risks, predict potential conjunctions, and develop avoidance maneuvers to protect satellites and spacecraft from debris collisions.

Moreover, digital platforms facilitate international collaboration and coordination in space debris mitigation efforts. Initiatives such as the Inter-Agency Space Debris Coordination Committee (IADC) and the

European Space Agency's Space Debris Office provide forums for space agencies and stakeholders to share data, exchange best practices, and coordinate debris mitigation strategies (Klinkrad, 2018). By leveraging digital communication networks and collaboration tools, countries can work together to develop common standards, guidelines, and regulations for responsible space behavior and debris mitigation.

Furthermore, digital technologies play a crucial role in space situational awareness (SSA) and space traffic management (STM) to prevent collisions and ensure safe operations in space. SSA systems, such as the United States Space Surveillance Network (SSN), track satellites, debris, and other objects in orbit to provide early warning of potential collisions and space hazards (Kelso et al., 2019). Digital tools and visualization platforms enable operators to analyze and interpret SSA data, assess collision risks, and make informed decisions to protect space assets and maintain orbital safety.

Additionally, digital platforms support cybersecurity initiatives to protect space assets, infrastructure, and communications systems from cyber threats and attacks. Digital encryption, authentication, and monitoring technologies help secure space-based networks, ground stations, and satellite operations against hacking, jamming, and interference (Weeden & Johnson-Freese, 2017). By implementing robust cybersecurity measures and information sharing protocols, spacefaring nations and organizations can enhance the resilience and integrity of space systems and operations in the face of evolving cyber threats.

However, addressing space debris and security challenges digitally also presents governance, policy, and regulatory considerations that must be addressed to ensure effectiveness and sustainability. International cooperation and coordination are essential to develop common standards, norms, and best practices for space debris mitigation, space traffic management, and cybersecurity in space (Diedrich & Rößler, 2021). Moreover, promoting transparency, accountability, and responsible behavior among space actors is crucial to prevent conflicts, accidents, and unintended consequences in the increasingly congested and contested space environment.

In conclusion, addressing space debris and security challenges digitally is essential for safeguarding space assets, ensuring orbital safety, and promoting responsible space behavior in the 21st century. By leveraging digital technologies, data analytics, and international cooperation, spacefaring nations and organizations can develop proactive strategies and solutions to mitigate the risks posed by space debris and enhance space security. However, addressing governance, policy, and regulatory considerations is essential to ensure the effectiveness, sustainability, and inclusivity of digital initiatives for space sustainability and security.

13.3 Promoting Peaceful Uses of Outer Space through Digital Diplomacy

Promoting peaceful uses of outer space through digital diplomacy represents a strategic approach to fostering collaboration, transparency, and trust among spacefaring nations and stakeholders in the increasingly complex and competitive space domain. By harnessing digital technologies, communication platforms, and international partnerships, countries can advance common interests, mitigate conflicts, and ensure the sustainable and equitable utilization of outer space for the benefit of all humanity (Jakhu & Pelton, 2018).

One of the primary ways digital diplomacy promotes peaceful uses of outer space is by facilitating dialogue, engagement, and cooperation among spacefaring nations and organizations. Digital communication platforms, such as virtual meetings, webinars, and online forums, provide opportunities for space agencies, policymakers, and experts to exchange ideas, share information, and discuss common challenges and opportunities in space exploration and utilization (Weeden & Johnson-Freese, 2020). By fostering open and transparent communication, digital diplomacy enhances understanding, builds confidence, and promotes collaboration in the global space community.

Moreover, digital diplomacy initiatives promote transparency, confidence-building measures, and space situational awareness to prevent misunderstandings, miscalculations, and conflicts in space. Digital platforms enable the sharing of data, information, and analyses on space activities, satellite orbits, and space traffic to enhance transparency and predictability in space operations (Gastrow, 2019). By promoting open access to space-related information and promoting responsible behavior, digital diplomacy fosters trust, reduces tensions, and strengthens stability in the space domain.

Furthermore, digital diplomacy supports the development of international norms, rules, and principles for responsible behavior in outer space. Initiatives such as the United Nations Committee on the Peaceful Uses of Outer Space (COPUOS) and the Group of Governmental Experts (GGE) on Transparency and Confidence-Building Measures in Outer Space provide forums for spacefaring nations to discuss and negotiate space governance issues (Hertzfeld & Preston, 2019). By leveraging digital tools and collaboration platforms, countries can work together to develop consensus-based guidelines, standards, and best practices that promote the peaceful and sustainable use of outer space.

Additionally, digital diplomacy initiatives engage non-state actors, civil society organizations, and the private sector in promoting peaceful uses of outer space and advancing common interests in space exploration and innovation. Digital platforms, social media campaigns, and online advocacy tools enable stakeholders to raise awareness, mobilize support, and advocate for policy reforms that promote transparency, cooperation, and sustainability in outer space activities (Cerruti, 2021). By fostering inclusive and participatory approaches to space governance, digital diplomacy empowers a diverse range of actors to contribute to shaping the future of space exploration and utilization.

However, promoting peaceful uses of outer space through digital diplomacy also faces challenges and obstacles that must be addressed to ensure effectiveness and sustainability. These include geopolitical tensions, competing interests, and divergent interpretations of space law and norms that may hinder cooperation and consensus-building in the global space community (Johnson-Freese, 2021). Moreover, ensuring equitable access to space resources, benefits, and opportunities is essential to avoid disparities and promote inclusivity in the space domain (Albinger, 2020). Digital diplomacy initiatives must prioritize diplomacy, dialogue, and cooperation to overcome challenges and promote peaceful uses of outer space for the benefit of present and future generations.

Promoting peaceful uses of outer space through digital diplomacy is essential for fostering cooperation, transparency, and trust in the increasingly complex and competitive space domain. By leveraging digital technologies, communication platforms, and international partnerships, countries can advance common interests, mitigate conflicts, and ensure the sustainable and equitable utilization of outer space. However, addressing challenges related to geopolitical tensions, inclusivity, and governance is essential to ensure the effectiveness and sustainability of digital diplomacy initiatives in promoting peace and security in outer space.

13.4 Space Governance and Policy Development in the Digital Age

Space governance and policy development in the digital age represent critical efforts to address the evolving challenges and opportunities in the rapidly expanding space domain. As nations and private entities increasingly venture into space exploration and utilization, the need for effective governance frameworks, regulatory mechanisms, and international cooperation becomes paramount to ensure the responsible and sustainable use of outer space (Frans von der Dunk, 2021).

One of the primary challenges in space governance in the digital age is the proliferation of space activities by an increasing number of actors, including governments, commercial entities, and non-state actors. Digital technologies have lowered barriers to entry into space, enabling smaller countries and private companies to launch satellites, conduct space missions, and engage in space commerce (Diedrich & Rößler, 2021). As a result, there is a growing need for updated governance structures and regulatory frameworks to address issues such as space traffic management, space debris mitigation, and space resource utilization in a comprehensive and equitable manner.

Moreover, digital technologies play a crucial role in enhancing transparency, accountability, and compliance monitoring in space activities. Space governance initiatives leverage digital tools, satellite tracking systems, and data analytics to monitor space operations, track satellite orbits, and assess compliance with international space law and regulations (Hertzfeld & Preston, 2019). By promoting transparency and information sharing, digital governance mechanisms facilitate confidence-building measures and promote responsible behavior in the global space community.

Furthermore, space governance in the digital age involves the development of international norms, rules, and principles for responsible behavior in outer space. Initiatives such as the United Nations Committee on the Peaceful Uses of Outer Space (COPUOS) and the Group of Governmental Experts (GGE) on Norms, Rules, and Principles of Behavior in Outer Space provide forums for countries to discuss and negotiate space governance issues (Johnson-Freese, 2020). By leveraging digital diplomacy and collaboration platforms, countries can work together to develop consensus-based guidelines, standards, and best practices that promote the peaceful and sustainable use of outer space.

Additionally, space governance in the digital age requires adaptation and innovation in legal and regulatory frameworks to keep pace with technological advancements and emerging challenges. Digital technologies such as blockchain, artificial intelligence, and remote sensing have the potential to transform space governance by enabling secure transactions, automated compliance monitoring, and enhanced situational awareness in space operations (Fricker et al., 2020). By harnessing these technologies, policymakers can develop agile and responsive regulatory regimes that promote innovation while ensuring safety, security, and sustainability in space activities.

However, space governance in the digital age also faces governance gaps, jurisdictional conflicts, and regulatory uncertainties that must be addressed to ensure effectiveness and inclusivity. The absence of a comprehensive international legal framework for space activities, coupled with divergent interpretations of space law and norms, poses challenges to harmonizing regulations and standards across countries (Jakhu & Pelton, 2018). Moreover, the rapid pace of technological change and the emergence of new actors in space raise questions about liability, accountability, and responsibility in the event of accidents or conflicts in space.

Space governance and policy development in the digital age are critical for addressing the evolving challenges and opportunities in the rapidly expanding space domain. By leveraging digital technologies, international cooperation, and innovative regulatory approaches, countries can develop effective governance frameworks that promote the peaceful, safe, and sustainable use of outer space. However, addressing governance gaps, jurisdictional conflicts, and regulatory uncertainties is essential to ensure the effectiveness and inclusivity of space governance mechanisms in the digital age.

14. Diaspora Diplomacy: Engaging Global Citizens through Digital Channels

"Diaspora diplomacy in the digital age offers unique opportunities to connect with global citizens, mobilize resources, and foster transnational networks for mutual benefit and development." - Robin Cohen

Diaspora diplomacy represents a strategic approach for governments and organizations to engage with their overseas communities to promote mutual understanding, cooperation, and development. In the digital age, advancements in communication technologies and social media platforms have transformed diaspora engagement, offering new opportunities for cross-border collaboration, networking, and advocacy (Gamlen, 2014).

One of the primary ways diaspora diplomacy engages global citizens through digital channels is by leveraging social media platforms, such as Facebook, Twitter, and WhatsApp, to connect with diaspora communities worldwide. Governments and organizations use these platforms to share news, updates, and opportunities with their diaspora members, fostering a sense of belonging and connection to their home countries (Bauböck & Faist, 2010). By engaging diaspora members in online conversations, governments can gather feedback, address concerns, and mobilize support for various initiatives, ranging from cultural exchanges to investment promotion.

Moreover, digital channels enable governments and organizations to organize virtual events, webinars, and online forums to facilitate dialogue and collaboration with diaspora communities. Virtual town halls, panel discussions, and networking sessions provide platforms for diaspora members to connect with each other, share experiences, and explore opportunities for collaboration and partnership (Levitt & Lamba-Nieves, 2011). By leveraging digital tools and platforms, governments and organizations can overcome geographic barriers and time constraints to engage diaspora communities in meaningful and inclusive ways.

Furthermore, diaspora diplomacy utilizes digital channels to mobilize resources, expertise, and support for development projects and initiatives in home countries. Crowdfunding platforms, online fundraising campaigns, and digital remittance services enable diaspora members to contribute financially to projects in their home countries, such as infrastructure development, education programs, and healthcare initiatives (Lahiri & Städler, 2019). By harnessing the collective power of diaspora networks and digital technologies, governments and organizations can catalyze development efforts and address pressing challenges in their home countries.

Additionally, digital channels provide platforms for diaspora members to advocate for policy changes, social justice issues, and human rights concerns in their home countries. Online petitions, social media campaigns, and digital advocacy tools enable diaspora communities to raise awareness, mobilize support, and amplify their voices on issues of importance to them (Bauböck & Smith, 2017). By engaging in digital advocacy, diaspora members can influence public opinion, shape policy debates, and drive positive change in their home countries.

However, diaspora diplomacy through digital channels also faces challenges and limitations that must be addressed to maximize its impact and effectiveness. These include digital divides, language barriers, and access constraints that may limit the participation of certain diaspora groups in online engagement efforts (Gamlen, 2008). Moreover, ensuring inclusivity, diversity, and representation within diaspora engagement initiatives is essential to avoid marginalizing certain voices and perspectives within diaspora communities (Levitt, 2017). Diaspora diplomacy efforts must be mindful of these challenges and work to overcome them through targeted outreach, capacity-building, and collaboration with diaspora organizations and networks.

Diaspora diplomacy engages global citizens through digital channels to promote cross-border collaboration, networking, and advocacy. By leveraging social media platforms, virtual events, and online advocacy tools, governments and organizations can connect with diaspora communities worldwide, mobilize resources for development projects, and amplify diaspora voices on issues of importance. However, addressing digital divides, language barriers, and inclusivity concerns is essential to ensure that diaspora diplomacy efforts are effective, inclusive, and impactful in engaging global citizens through digital channels.

14.1 Harnessing the Power of Diaspora Communities for Diplomatic Outreach

Harnessing the power of diaspora communities for diplomatic outreach represents a strategic approach for governments to extend their influence, promote their interests, and foster collaboration across borders. In the digital age, leveraging the connectivity and networks of diaspora communities through digital engagement initiatives offers unprecedented opportunities for diplomatic engagement, cultural exchange, and economic cooperation (Gamlen, 2014).

One of the primary ways governments harness the power of diaspora communities for diplomatic outreach is by establishing digital platforms and online networks to connect with diaspora members worldwide. Websites, social media pages, and online forums provide channels for governments to share information, updates, and initiatives with diaspora communities, fostering a sense of belonging and connection to their home countries (Levitt & Lamba-Nieves, 2011). By engaging diaspora members in online conversations, governments can gather insights, address concerns, and mobilize support for diplomatic efforts and initiatives.

Moreover, diplomatic missions and consulates leverage digital channels to organize virtual events, webinars, and cultural exchanges to engage with diaspora communities and strengthen bilateral relations. Virtual town halls, panel discussions, and networking sessions enable diplomats to interact with diaspora members, share perspectives, and explore opportunities for collaboration and partnership (Bauböck & Faist, 2010). By leveraging digital tools and platforms, diplomatic missions can overcome geographic barriers and time constraints to engage diaspora communities in meaningful and inclusive ways.

Furthermore, governments harness the expertise, resources, and networks of diaspora communities to advance diplomatic objectives, promote economic development, and foster innovation in their home countries. Diaspora members often possess valuable skills, knowledge, and connections that can contribute to diplomatic initiatives, trade promotion efforts, and investment projects (Lahiri & Städler, 2019). By engaging diaspora communities as strategic partners and stakeholders, governments can leverage their expertise and networks to advance mutual interests and achieve diplomatic goals.

Additionally, digital engagement initiatives enable governments to mobilize diaspora communities to advocate for policy changes, promote cultural diplomacy, and support humanitarian efforts in their home countries. Online petitions, social media campaigns, and digital advocacy tools empower diaspora members to raise awareness, mobilize support, and amplify their voices on issues of importance to them and their communities (Bauböck & Smith, 2017). By harnessing the collective power of diaspora networks and digital technologies, governments can amplify their diplomatic efforts and drive positive change in their home countries.

However, harnessing the power of diaspora communities for diplomatic outreach also presents challenges and considerations that must be addressed to ensure effectiveness and inclusivity. These include cultural sensitivities, language barriers, and diaspora diversity, which may require tailored approaches and targeted engagement strategies (Levitt, 2017). Moreover, ensuring transparency, accountability, and inclusivity in diplomatic outreach efforts is essential to build trust and foster meaningful collaboration with diaspora communities (Gamlen, 2008). Diplomatic missions must be mindful of these challenges and work collaboratively with diaspora organizations and networks to overcome them and maximize the impact of their engagement efforts.

Harnessing the power of diaspora communities for diplomatic outreach offers governments unique opportunities to extend their influence, promote their interests, and strengthen bilateral relations. By leveraging digital engagement initiatives, governments can connect with diaspora communities worldwide, organize virtual events, and mobilize support for diplomatic initiatives and projects. However, addressing cultural sensitivities, language barriers, and diversity considerations is essential to ensure that diplomatic outreach efforts are inclusive, effective, and impactful in engaging diaspora communities and advancing mutual interests.

14.2 Providing Consular Services and Support Digitally

Providing consular services and support digitally represents a transformative approach for governments to meet the needs of their diaspora communities, offering convenience, accessibility, and efficiency in accessing essential services and assistance. In the digital age, advancements in technology and communication platforms have revolutionized the way consular services are delivered, enabling governments to reach diaspora members worldwide and offer a wide range of services remotely (Aronoff & Orrenius, 2016).

One of the primary ways governments provide consular services and support digitally is through online portals and mobile applications that offer a range of services, including passport renewal, visa applications, and notary services. These digital platforms provide diaspora members with convenient access to consular services from anywhere in the world, reducing the need for in-person visits to embassies or consulates (Choucri & Goldsmith, 2012). By streamlining processes and reducing administrative burdens, digital consular services enhance efficiency and responsiveness in serving diaspora communities.

Moreover, governments leverage digital communication channels, such as email, chatbots, and social media, to provide real-time assistance and support to diaspora members facing emergencies, crises, or consular issues. Consular officials use digital platforms to communicate with diaspora members, provide information, and offer assistance in navigating complex situations, such as medical emergencies, natural disasters, or legal challenges (Aroca & Stalker, 2015). By offering personalized support and guidance digitally, governments can ensure timely and effective assistance to diaspora communities in times of need.

Furthermore, digital consular services facilitate outreach and engagement with diaspora communities through virtual town halls, webinars, and online forums. Consular officials organize virtual events to provide updates on consular services, address frequently asked questions, and engage with diaspora members on issues of interest or concern (Ozkirimli, 2010). By leveraging digital platforms for outreach and engagement, governments can foster stronger ties with diaspora communities, build trust, and demonstrate their commitment to serving their citizens abroad.

Additionally, governments use digital platforms to provide consular information and resources to diaspora communities, including travel advisories, safety alerts, and legal guidance. Consular websites and social media channels serve as valuable sources of information for diaspora members seeking guidance on travel regulations, entry requirements, and consular assistance procedures (Aroca & Stalker, 2015). By offering up-to-date information and resources digitally, governments can empower diaspora communities to make informed decisions and access the support they need when traveling or living abroad.

However, providing consular services and support digitally also presents challenges and considerations that governments must address to ensure effectiveness and inclusivity. These include digital divides, language barriers, and accessibility issues that may limit the ability of certain diaspora groups to access digital services (Choucri & Goldsmith, 2012). Moreover, ensuring data privacy, security, and confidentiality in digital consular services is essential to protect the personal information and rights of diaspora members (Aronoff & Orrenius, 2016). Governments must prioritize inclusivity, accessibility, and data security in designing and delivering digital consular services to ensure that all diaspora members can access the support they need effectively and securely.

rPoviding consular services and support digitally offers governments a powerful tool to enhance access, efficiency, and responsiveness in serving their diaspora communities. By leveraging online portals, digital communication channels, and virtual engagement initiatives, governments can offer a wide range of consular services remotely, reach diaspora members worldwide, and provide timely assistance and support in times of need. However, addressing digital divides, accessibility concerns, and data security considerations is essential to ensure that digital consular services are inclusive, effective, and trustworthy in serving diaspora communities.

14.3 Leveraging Diaspora Networks for Economic and Cultural Diplomacy

Leveraging diaspora networks for economic and cultural diplomacy represents a strategic approach for governments to foster economic growth, promote cultural exchange, and strengthen bilateral relations with their diaspora communities and host countries. In the digital age, advancements in technology and communication have facilitated closer connections and collaboration between diaspora members and their countries of origin, offering new opportunities for economic partnerships and cultural exchange (Gamlen, 2014).

One of the primary ways governments leverage diaspora networks for economic diplomacy is by promoting investment, trade, and entrepreneurship initiatives targeting diaspora members and their networks. Governments organize investment forums, business matchmaking events, and entrepreneurship programs to connect diaspora entrepreneurs with investment opportunities and business partnerships in their home countries (Lahiri & Städler, 2019). By leveraging diaspora networks, governments can attract foreign direct investment, stimulate economic development, and create job opportunities in key sectors such as technology, finance, and tourism.

Moreover, governments collaborate with diaspora communities to promote trade and exports of goods and services between their home countries and host countries. Trade missions, export promotion campaigns, and business delegations facilitate market access and networking opportunities for diaspora businesses and exporters (Bauböck & Faist, 2010). By leveraging diaspora networks as market intermediaries and cultural brokers, governments can enhance trade relations, facilitate cross-border commerce, and diversify export markets for their goods and services.

Furthermore, governments harness diaspora networks for cultural diplomacy initiatives aimed at promoting their countries' cultural heritage, traditions, and soft power abroad. Cultural festivals, art exhibitions, and performing arts events showcase the richness and diversity of the diaspora's cultural contributions to host countries and global audiences (Aroca & Stalker, 2015). By engaging diaspora artists, writers, and cultural ambassadors, governments can enhance their countries' cultural influence, foster intercultural dialogue, and strengthen people-to-people ties across borders.

Additionally, governments collaborate with diaspora communities to promote educational and academic partnerships, research collaborations, and knowledge exchange initiatives. Diaspora members often serve as bridges between academic institutions, research centers, and innovation hubs in their home countries and host countries, facilitating collaboration and technology transfer (Choucri & Goldsmith, 2012). By leveraging diaspora expertise and networks, governments can promote innovation, research excellence, and human capital development in key sectors such as science, technology, and education.

However, leveraging diaspora networks for economic and cultural diplomacy also presents challenges and considerations that governments must address to ensure effectiveness and sustainability. These include diaspora diversity, fragmentation, and competing interests that may require tailored approaches and targeted engagement strategies (Gamlen, 2008). Moreover, ensuring transparency, accountability, and inclusivity in economic and cultural diplomacy initiatives is essential to build trust and foster meaningful collaboration with diaspora communities (Aronoff & Orrenius, 2016). Governments must prioritize dialogue, partnership, and mutual respect in leveraging diaspora networks for economic and cultural diplomacy to maximize their impact and effectiveness.

Everaging diaspora networks for economic and cultural diplomacy offers governments a strategic approach to promote economic growth, cultural exchange, and bilateral relations with their diaspora communities and host countries. By engaging diaspora members as partners and stakeholders in economic and cultural initiatives, governments can stimulate investment, trade, and entrepreneurship, promote cultural heritage and soft power, and strengthen people-to-people ties across borders. However, addressing diaspora diversity, engagement challenges, and governance considerations is essential to ensure that economic and cultural diplomacy initiatives are inclusive, effective, and sustainable in leveraging diaspora networks for mutual prosperity and understanding.

14.4 Addressing Challenges and Opportunities in Diaspora Engagement Online

Addressing challenges and opportunities in diaspora engagement online is essential for governments seeking to effectively connect with and mobilize their diaspora communities in the digital age. While digital platforms offer unprecedented opportunities for engagement, they also present unique challenges that governments must navigate to ensure meaningful interaction, inclusivity, and impact (Gamlen, 2014).

One of the primary challenges in diaspora engagement online is overcoming digital divides and accessibility barriers that may limit the participation of certain segments of the diaspora community. Not all members may have equal access to the internet, digital literacy skills, or familiarity with online platforms (Aroca & Stalker, 2015). Governments must adopt inclusive approaches and provide support and resources to ensure that all members of the diaspora can access and participate in online engagement initiatives.

Moreover, language barriers pose another challenge in diaspora engagement online, as members may speak different languages and dialects. Governments must provide multilingual content and communication channels to ensure that information and engagement opportunities are accessible to all members of the diaspora community (Bauböck & Faist, 2010). Translation services, language-specific social media accounts, and localized websites can help overcome language barriers and enhance engagement with diverse diaspora groups.

Furthermore, ensuring authenticity, trust, and credibility in online engagement initiatives is essential to build meaningful relationships and foster trust with diaspora communities. Governments must be transparent, responsive, and accountable in their online interactions, addressing concerns, feedback, and queries in a timely and respectful manner (Choucri & Goldsmith, 2012). Authentic engagement requires listening to the voices of the diaspora, valuing their perspectives, and incorporating their feedback into policymaking and decision-making processes.

Additionally, governments must navigate the complex landscape of social media and digital communication platforms to effectively engage diaspora communities online. Each platform has its own dynamics, norms, and audience preferences, requiring tailored strategies and approaches for engagement (Aronoff & Orrenius, 2016). Governments must invest in digital diplomacy capabilities, train diplomatic staff in social media management and online engagement, and adapt their communication strategies to the evolving digital landscape.

Moreover, protecting data privacy, security, and confidentiality is essential in diaspora engagement online to safeguard the personal information and rights of diaspora members (Lahiri & Städler, 2019). Governments must comply with data protection regulations, implement robust cybersecurity measures, and ensure that online engagement platforms are secure and trustworthy (Gamlen, 2008). Building trust and confidence in online engagement initiatives requires transparency, accountability, and respect for the privacy and security concerns of diaspora communities.

Despite these challenges, diaspora engagement online also offers significant opportunities for governments to connect with and mobilize their diaspora communities in meaningful and impactful ways. Digital platforms enable governments to reach diaspora members worldwide, facilitate dialogue and collaboration, and mobilize support for diplomatic, economic, and cultural initiatives (Bauböck & Smith, 2017). By leveraging digital diplomacy strategies, governments can overcome barriers, seize opportunities, and strengthen relationships with their diaspora communities in the digital age.

In conclusion, addressing challenges and opportunities in diaspora engagement online requires governments to adopt inclusive, authentic, and responsive approaches to digital diplomacy. By overcoming digital divides, language barriers, and trust issues, governments can effectively engage diaspora communities online, build meaningful relationships, and mobilize support for diplomatic, economic, and cultural initiatives. However, navigating the complexities of social media, protecting data privacy and security, and ensuring authenticity and trustworthiness are essential for successful diaspora engagement online in the digital age.

Part III
Future Trends of Digital Diplomacy

15. The Future of Digital Diplomacy: Trends and Forecasts

"In the digital age, diplomacy must adapt. It's not just about what happens behind closed doors; it's about the conversations happening in the open online space." - Ban Ki-moon

As we navigate the future of digital diplomacy, several key trends and forecasts are shaping the landscape of international relations, communication, and engagement. In the era of rapid technological advancement and globalization, digital diplomacy is evolving to meet the changing needs and dynamics of diplomatic practice (Sevin & Ba, 2018).

One prominent trend in the future of digital diplomacy is the increasing use of artificial intelligence (AI) and data analytics to enhance diplomatic decision-making, communication strategies, and public engagement efforts. AI-powered tools, such as natural language processing and sentiment analysis, enable diplomats to analyze large volumes of data from social media, news sources, and public opinion to gain insights into global trends, sentiments, and perceptions (Merlingen & Ojanen, 2020). By leveraging AI, diplomats can tailor their messaging, target audiences more effectively, and anticipate emerging issues and crises in real-time.

Moreover, the future of digital diplomacy will see the continued integration of virtual reality (VR) and augmented reality (AR) technologies to enhance diplomatic training, cultural exchange, and public diplomacy initiatives. VR simulations and AR applications enable diplomats to immerse themselves in virtual environments, conduct virtual meetings and conferences, and engage with stakeholders in innovative ways (Cull & Koenig, 2017). By leveraging VR and AR, diplomats can transcend geographical barriers, foster cross-cultural understanding, and build bridges between people and nations.

Furthermore, the future of digital diplomacy will witness the growing importance of cybersecurity and digital resilience in diplomatic practice. As cyber threats and disinformation campaigns become increasingly sophisticated and pervasive, diplomats must prioritize cybersecurity measures, data protection protocols, and resilience strategies to safeguard diplomatic communications and information (Fisch, 2020). By investing in cybersecurity capabilities, diplomatic missions can mitigate risks, protect sensitive data, and uphold the integrity and trustworthiness of digital diplomacy initiatives.

Additionally, the future of digital diplomacy will see the rise of multi-stakeholder partnerships and collaboration platforms to address global challenges and advance shared goals. Diplomats, civil society organizations, private sector actors, and technology companies will collaborate on digital diplomacy initiatives ranging from climate action to public health to human rights (Kurbalija & Katrandjiev, 2018). By fostering inclusive and participatory approaches to digital diplomacy, stakeholders can leverage collective expertise, resources, and networks to achieve meaningful impact and sustainable outcomes.

Moreover, the future of digital diplomacy will be characterized by the proliferation of diplomatic innovation labs, incubators, and experimentation platforms to foster creativity, innovation, and adaptive learning in diplomatic practice. Diplomatic institutions and think tanks will establish dedicated innovation hubs to explore emerging technologies, experiment with new communication tools, and co-create solutions to diplomatic challenges (Shaikh, 2019). By fostering a culture of innovation and experimentation, diplomats can adapt to changing environments, seize opportunities, and drive positive change in the digital age.

The future of digital diplomacy is characterized by emerging trends and forecasts that are reshaping the practice of diplomacy in profound ways. From the integration of AI and data analytics to the use of VR and AR technologies, from cybersecurity and digital resilience to multi-stakeholder collaboration and diplomatic innovation, the future of digital diplomacy holds immense potential for diplomats to navigate complex challenges and seize opportunities in an interconnected and rapidly changing world.

15.1 Emerging Technologies and Their Impact on Diplomatic Practice

Emerging technologies are revolutionizing diplomatic practice, offering new tools and capabilities to diplomats to engage, communicate, and collaborate in the digital age. As diplomats adapt to the changing landscape of international relations, several key emerging technologies are reshaping diplomatic practice and strategy (Kurbalija & Katrandjiev, 2018).

One significant emerging technology impacting diplomatic practice is artificial intelligence (AI), which is transforming diplomatic decision-making, analysis, and communication. AI-powered tools enable diplomats to analyze vast amounts of data, identify patterns, and gain insights into global trends and sentiments (Merlingen & Ojanen, 2020). AI algorithms can assist diplomats in predicting crises, tailoring communication strategies, and identifying opportunities for collaboration and conflict resolution.

Moreover, virtual reality (VR) and augmented reality (AR) technologies are revolutionizing diplomatic training, cultural exchange, and public engagement efforts. VR simulations and AR applications enable diplomats to immerse themselves in virtual environments, conduct virtual meetings and conferences, and interact with stakeholders in innovative ways (Cull & Koenig, 2017). By leveraging VR and AR, diplomats can foster cross-cultural understanding, bridge geographical divides, and enhance diplomatic engagement and outreach.

Furthermore, blockchain technology is transforming diplomatic communication, information sharing, and trust-building initiatives. Blockchain enables secure and transparent transactions, data verification, and digital identity management, enhancing the integrity and reliability of diplomatic communications (Nasiri, 2019). Diplomatic missions are exploring blockchain applications for secure document exchange, consular services, and diplomatic negotiations, improving efficiency and accountability in diplomatic practice.

Additionally, big data analytics and predictive modeling are empowering diplomats to anticipate and respond to emerging challenges and opportunities in real-time. By analyzing social media data, news sources, and public opinion, diplomats can monitor global trends, assess public sentiment, and tailor their communication strategies accordingly (Khan, 2021). Big data analytics enable diplomats to identify emerging issues, detect misinformation campaigns, and engage with stakeholders proactively to address pressing

15.2. Predictive Analytics and Big Data in Diplomatic Decision-Making

Predictive analytics and big data are poised to revolutionize diplomatic decision-making processes, offering diplomats powerful tools for forecasting trends, assessing risks, and informing policy formulation. This section explores the potential impact of predictive analytics and big data on diplomatic practice and their implications for international relations.

Predictive analytics involves the use of statistical algorithms and machine learning techniques to analyze historical data and predict future outcomes or trends. In the context of diplomacy, predictive analytics enables diplomats to anticipate diplomatic challenges, identify emerging trends, and forecast potential crises (Council on Foreign Relations, 2020). By leveraging large datasets from diverse sources such as social media, news articles, and diplomatic cables, diplomats can gain insights into public sentiment, geopolitical developments, and policy dynamics, thereby enhancing their strategic foresight and decision-making capabilities.

Big data refers to the vast volumes of structured and unstructured data generated from various sources, including social media platforms, sensors, and digital devices. Diplomatic institutions can harness big data analytics to extract valuable insights and patterns from these datasets, enabling diplomats to make evidence-based policy recommendations and diplomatic strategies (Ministry of Foreign Affairs of Denmark, 2020). Big data analytics can reveal hidden correlations, uncover causal relationships, and provide diplomats with a deeper understanding of complex diplomatic issues, facilitating more informed and effective decision-making.

The integration of predictive analytics and big data in diplomatic decision-making processes offers diplomats several benefits. Firstly, it enhances diplomats' situational awareness by providing real-time intelligence and analysis of global developments (European External Action Service, 2021). By monitoring social media trends, tracking news headlines, and analyzing diplomatic communications, diplomats can stay abreast of evolving dynamics and respond promptly to emerging challenges. Secondly, it enables diplomats to identify opportunities for diplomatic engagement and collaboration by identifying areas of common interest and convergence among states and stakeholders (United Nations Department of Economic and Social Affairs, 2020). By leveraging big data analytics, diplomats can identify potential allies, anticipate diplomatic openings, and devise diplomatic initiatives to advance shared interests and objectives.

However, the adoption of predictive analytics and big data in diplomatic decision-making also poses challenges and considerations. Diplomatic institutions must ensure the accuracy, reliability, and ethical use of data to mitigate the risk of bias or misinformation (Council of Europe, 2021). Moreover, concerns regarding data privacy, cybersecurity, and information sharing may arise, particularly in the context of sensitive diplomatic negotiations and confidential communications (United

Nations Institute for Training and Research, 2019). Diplomatic practitioners must navigate these challenges carefully and implement robust governance frameworks to safeguard data integrity, protect privacy rights, and uphold ethical standards in the use of predictive analytics and big data.

Predictive analytics and big data hold immense promise for enhancing diplomatic decision-making processes and advancing international relations. By harnessing the power of predictive analytics and big data analytics, diplomats can gain deeper insights into global trends, anticipate diplomatic challenges, and identify opportunities for cooperation. However, the responsible and ethical use of predictive analytics and big data is essential to ensure the integrity, transparency, and credibility of diplomatic decision-making processes in the digital age.

15.3 Artificial Intelligence and Machine Learning in Diplomatic Processes

Artificial intelligence (AI) and machine learning (ML) technologies are poised to revolutionize diplomatic processes, offering diplomats powerful tools for analysis, decision-making support, and automation. This section explores the potential applications of AI and ML in diplomatic practice and their implications for international relations.

AI refers to the simulation of human intelligence processes by machines, while ML is a subset of AI that enables machines to learn from data and improve their performance over time without explicit programming. In the context of diplomacy, AI and ML technologies can be leveraged to automate routine tasks, analyze vast datasets, and generate actionable insights to inform diplomatic strategies and policies (Ministry of Foreign Affairs of the Netherlands, 2020). For example, AI-powered natural language processing (NLP) algorithms can analyze diplomatic documents, speeches, and communications to extract key themes, sentiments, and trends, providing diplomats with valuable intelligence for decision-making.

One of the key applications of AI and ML in diplomatic processes is in the field of diplomacy, where AI-driven algorithms can analyze diplomatic communications, detect patterns, and predict diplomatic outcomes (Council on Foreign Relations, 2020). By analyzing historical diplomatic negotiations and agreements, ML algorithms can identify common negotiation tactics, assess negotiation dynamics, and generate predictive models to anticipate negotiation outcomes. This enables diplomats to develop more effective negotiation strategies, identify potential areas of compromise, and optimize diplomatic outcomes.

Another area where AI and ML technologies can enhance diplomatic processes is in crisis management and conflict resolution. AI-driven analytics tools can analyze social media feeds, news articles, and other sources of information to detect early warning signs of conflict, identify potential hotspots, and predict escalation dynamics (United Nations Department of Economic and Social Affairs, 2020). By leveraging AI-generated insights, diplomats can proactively engage in preventive diplomacy, mediate disputes, and de-escalate tensions before they escalate into full-blown conflicts.

Furthermore, AI and ML technologies can facilitate cross-cultural communication and understanding by providing diplomats with language translation and interpretation tools (European External Action Service, 2021). AI-powered translation algorithms can translate diplomatic documents, speeches, and communications in real-time, enabling diplomats to communicate more effectively with their counterparts from different linguistic and cultural backgrounds. This enhances diplomatic engagement, fosters mutual understanding, and promotes dialogue and cooperation in international relations.

However, the adoption of AI and ML in diplomatic processes also raises ethical, legal, and practical considerations. Diplomatic institutions must ensure the transparency, accountability, and fairness of AI algorithms to mitigate the risk of bias or discrimination (Council of Europe, 2021). Moreover, concerns regarding data privacy, cybersecurity, and information security must be addressed to safeguard sensitive diplomatic communications and ensure the integrity of diplomatic processes (United Nations Institute for Training and Research, 2019). Diplomatic practitioners must navigate these challenges carefully and implement robust governance frameworks to uphold ethical standards and protect diplomatic interests in the use of AI and ML technologies.

AI and ML technologies offer diplomats unprecedented opportunities to enhance diplomatic processes, improve decision-making, and advance international relations. By harnessing the power of AI and ML, diplomats can gain deeper insights into diplomatic dynamics, predict diplomatic outcomes, and facilitate conflict resolution and crisis management. However, the responsible and ethical use of AI and ML is essential to ensure the integrity, transparency, and credibility of diplomatic processes in the digital age.

15.4. Ethical and Strategic Implications of Emerging Technologies in Digital Diplomacy

The integration of emerging technologies in digital diplomacy brings about ethical and strategic considerations that diplomats and diplomatic institutions must carefully navigate. This section explores the ethical and strategic implications of leveraging emerging technologies in diplomatic practice and their broader impact on international relations.

Ethical Implications:

Data Privacy and Security: *The use of emerging technologies such as AI, big data, and VR raises concerns about data privacy and security.*

Diplomatic institutions must ensure the responsible and transparent handling of diplomatic data to protect sensitive information and uphold diplomats' privacy rights (Council of Europe, 2021). Robust cybersecurity measures are essential to safeguard diplomatic communications and prevent unauthorized access or manipulation of diplomatic data.

Bias and Discrimination*: AI algorithms and machine learning models are susceptible to biases inherent in the data used for training. Diplomatic institutions must mitigate the risk of bias and discrimination in AI-driven decision-making processes to ensure fairness and equity in diplomatic outcomes (European External Action Service, 2021). Ethical AI frameworks and diversity-aware algorithms can help address biases and promote inclusivity in diplomatic practices.*

Digital Divide: *The adoption of emerging technologies in digital diplomacy may exacerbate existing inequalities in access to technology and digital literacy. Diplomatic institutions must address the digital divide by providing equitable access to training, resources, and infrastructure for diplomats worldwide (United Nations Educational, Scientific and Cultural Organization [UNESCO], 2020). Bridging the digital divide ensures that all diplomats can participate fully in digital diplomacy initiatives and benefit from the opportunities afforded by emerging technologies.*

Strategic Implications:

Geopolitical Competition: *Emerging technologies in digital diplomacy are increasingly shaping geopolitical dynamics and competition among states. Diplomatic institutions must navigate the geopolitical landscape carefully and assess the strategic implications of technological advancements on international relations (Ministry of Foreign Affairs of Denmark, 2020). Strategic foresight and diplomatic agility are crucial for diplomats to anticipate geopolitical shifts, adapt to emerging challenges, and leverage technological innovations to advance national interests and objectives.*

Soft Power Projection: *The use of emerging technologies offers diplomats new avenues for projecting soft power and shaping international perceptions. Virtual diplomacy initiatives, social media engagement, and cultural exchanges facilitated by emerging technologies enable diplomats to showcase their country's values, culture, and diplomatic prowess on the global stage (Ministry of Foreign Affairs of Japan, 2019). Strategic communication strategies and digital branding efforts play a crucial role in enhancing a country's soft power and influence in the digital age.*

Norm Setting and Diplomatic Cooperation: *Diplomatic institutions play a key role in shaping international norms and rules governing the use of emerging technologies in diplomacy. Diplomatic cooperation and multilateral engagement are essential for establishing common standards, norms, and regulations to govern the responsible and ethical use of emerging technologies (United Nations Department of Economic and Social Affairs, 2020). Diplomats must engage in dialogue and negotiation with other states and stakeholders to build consensus and foster cooperation in addressing emerging challenges and opportunities in the digital domain.*

The adoption of emerging technologies in digital diplomacy brings about both ethical and strategic implications that diplomats and diplomatic institutions must address proactively. By upholding ethical principles, promoting inclusivity, and safeguarding privacy and security, diplomats can ensure the responsible use of emerging technologies in diplomatic practice. Moreover, by navigating geopolitical competition, projecting soft power, and fostering diplomatic cooperation, diplomats can leverage emerging technologies to advance national interests and contribute to the stability and prosperity of the international community.

15.5 Shifting Geopolitical Dynamics and Digital Diplomacy

Shifting geopolitical dynamics are profoundly influencing the practice of digital diplomacy, shaping how nations engage, cooperate, and compete in the digital domain. As traditional power structures evolve and new challenges emerge, digital diplomacy is becoming increasingly integral to navigating complex geopolitical landscapes (Kurbalija & Katrandjiev, 2018).

One significant aspect of shifting geopolitical dynamics is the rise of digital authoritarianism and the proliferation of cyber threats, disinformation campaigns, and online censorship by authoritarian regimes. Digital diplomacy plays a crucial role in countering these challenges by promoting internet freedom, defending human rights online, and advocating for democratic values and principles (Fischer, 2020). Through digital outreach, diplomatic missions can raise awareness, mobilize support, and build coalitions to push back against digital authoritarianism and protect the open and secure internet.

Furthermore, shifting geopolitical dynamics are reshaping alliances and partnerships in the digital realm, as nations seek to forge strategic alliances, enhance cybersecurity cooperation, and promote digital trade and innovation (Merlingen & Ojanen, 2020). Digital diplomacy enables diplomats to engage with a diverse range of stakeholders, including governments, civil society organizations, and private sector actors, to address shared challenges such as cyber threats, disinformation, and data privacy breaches. By fostering dialogue and collaboration, digital diplomacy can strengthen trust, build resilience, and promote stability in an increasingly interconnected world.

Moreover, shifting geopolitical dynamics are influencing the role of digital diplomacy in conflict resolution, crisis management, and peacebuilding efforts. Digital platforms provide channels for diplomatic communication, mediation, and negotiation, enabling diplomats to engage with conflicting parties, facilitate dialogue, and seek peaceful resolutions to conflicts (Sevin & Ba, 2018). Through digital mediation and track-two diplomacy initiatives, diplomats can bridge divides, build trust, and lay the groundwork for sustainable peace agreements in conflict-affected regions.

Additionally, shifting geopolitical dynamics are driving the digitalization of traditional diplomatic practices, as nations adapt to new communication technologies, social media platforms, and digital engagement tools (Cull & Koenig, 2017). Digital diplomacy offers diplomats unprecedented opportunities to engage directly with foreign publics, shape public opinion, and influence perceptions of their countries abroad. By leveraging digital storytelling, social media campaigns, and virtual engagement initiatives, diplomats can enhance their countries' soft power, project positive narratives, and build goodwill with global audiences.

Shifting geopolitical dynamics are reshaping the practice of digital diplomacy, presenting both opportunities and challenges for nations navigating complex international landscapes. By countering digital authoritarianism, fostering strategic partnerships, promoting conflict resolution, and embracing digital innovation, digital diplomacy can play a crucial role in advancing national interests, promoting stability, and addressing global challenges in the digital age.

15.6 The Role of Non-State Actors in Shaping Digital Diplomacy

Non-state actors play an increasingly influential role in shaping digital diplomacy, challenging traditional diplomatic practices and institutions, and amplifying voices beyond government channels. As digital technologies empower individuals, civil society organizations, and private sector actors to engage in diplomatic activities, the landscape of diplomacy is undergoing significant transformation (Fisher, 2020).

One significant aspect of the role of non-state actors in shaping digital diplomacy is their capacity to drive public diplomacy and shape international perceptions through digital platforms and social media channels. Non-governmental organizations (NGOs), advocacy groups, and grassroots movements use digital tools to raise awareness, mobilize support, and influence public opinion on global issues such as human rights, climate change, and social justice (Sarhan, 2018). By leveraging social media campaigns, online petitions, and digital advocacy initiatives, non-state actors can amplify their voices and push governments to take action on key diplomatic priorities.

Moreover, non-state actors are increasingly engaging in track-two diplomacy and informal dialogue initiatives to complement and sometimes challenge official diplomatic efforts. Academic institutions, think tanks, and research organizations organize digital conferences, workshops, and expert roundtables to facilitate dialogue, build trust, and generate innovative solutions to diplomatic challenges (Kurbalija & Katrandjiev, 2018). By providing neutral platforms for dialogue and collaboration, non-state actors contribute to building bridges between conflicting parties and advancing diplomatic goals in conflict-affected regions.

Furthermore, non-state actors play a crucial role in promoting digital innovation and technological cooperation in diplomatic practice. Technology companies, startups, and innovation hubs develop digital solutions, tools, and platforms that enhance diplomatic communication, crisis response, and public engagement (Fischer, 2020). By partnering with non-state actors, diplomatic missions can access cutting-edge technology, leverage expertise, and embrace digital innovation to enhance their diplomatic capabilities and effectiveness in the digital age.

Additionally, non-state actors are at the forefront of promoting cybersecurity, digital rights, and internet governance in diplomatic discourse. Civil society organizations, internet activists, and human rights defenders advocate for policies and regulations that protect online freedoms, privacy rights, and cybersecurity (Sarhan, 2018). By engaging with non-state actors, governments can gain valuable insights, perspectives, and expertise on digital issues, inform policymaking processes, and ensure that diplomatic initiatives uphold democratic values and principles in the digital domain.

In conclusion, non-state actors play a multifaceted role in shaping digital diplomacy, complementing and sometimes challenging traditional diplomatic practices and institutions. By driving public diplomacy, engaging in track-two diplomacy, promoting digital innovation, and advocating for digital rights, non-state actors contribute to advancing diplomatic goals, fostering dialogue, and addressing global challenges in the digital age. Embracing collaboration and partnership with non-state actors is essential for governments to harness the full potential of digital diplomacy and navigate complex international landscapes effectively.

15.7. Anticipating Challenges and Seizing Opportunities in the Future Digital Landscape

As we look ahead to the future digital diplomatic landscape, it is crucial to anticipate the challenges and opportunities that will shape diplomatic practice in the years to come. From emerging technologies to shifting geopolitical dynamics, diplomats must navigate a complex and rapidly evolving landscape to effectively advance their countries' interests and address global challenges (Kurbalija & Katrandjiev, 2018).

One significant challenge in the future digital diplomatic landscape is the proliferation of cyber threats, disinformation campaigns, and digital authoritarianism by state and non-state actors. Diplomats must adapt to new cyber realities, develop cybersecurity capabilities, and enhance resilience against cyber attacks and information warfare (Fischer, 2020). By investing in cybersecurity measures, fostering international cooperation, and promoting norms and standards in cyberspace, diplomats can mitigate risks and protect the integrity of digital diplomacy initiatives.

Moreover, diplomats must grapple with the ethical and regulatory implications of emerging technologies such as artificial intelligence (AI), biotechnology, and quantum computing. AI-powered algorithms raise concerns about bias, privacy, and accountability in decision-making processes, while biotechnological advancements raise ethical dilemmas around genetic engineering and biosecurity (Merlingen & Ojanen, 2020). Diplomats must engage in multilateral dialogues, negotiate international agreements, and develop ethical frameworks to govern the responsible use of emerging technologies and ensure that they benefit humanity.

Furthermore, diplomats must address digital divides, access disparities, and inequalities in the future digital landscape to ensure that all nations and communities can harness the benefits of digital technologies. The digital divide between developed and developing countries, as well as within countries, exacerbates social and economic inequalities and limits opportunities for inclusive development (Sevin & Ba, 2018). Diplomats must prioritize digital inclusion, capacity-building, and technology transfer initiatives to bridge divides, empower marginalized communities, and promote sustainable development in the digital age.

Additionally, diplomats must navigate the geopolitical implications of digital globalization, as digital technologies transcend national borders and reshape traditional power dynamics. The rise of digital platforms, data flows, and transnational networks challenge traditional notions of sovereignty, territoriality, and jurisdiction (Kurbalija & Katrandjiev, 2018). Diplomats must negotiate new rules and norms in cyberspace, address cross-border challenges such as cybercrime and data privacy breaches, and promote cooperation and coordination among nations to ensure a stable and secure digital environment.

Despite these challenges, the future digital diplomatic landscape also presents significant opportunities for diplomats to advance their countries' interests and address global challenges effectively. Digital technologies offer new channels for diplomacy, communication, and engagement, enabling diplomats to reach wider audiences, foster dialogue, and mobilize support for diplomatic initiatives (Fischer, 2020). By embracing innovation, collaboration, and adaptability, diplomats can seize opportunities to shape the future digital landscape in ways that promote peace, prosperity, and human dignity.

Anticipating challenges and seizing opportunities in the future digital diplomatic landscape requires diplomats to adopt forward-looking strategies, embrace digital innovation, and engage in multistakeholder dialogue and cooperation. By addressing cyber threats, navigating ethical dilemmas, promoting digital inclusion, and navigating geopolitical complexities, diplomats can harness the transformative potential of digital technologies to advance their countries' interests and contribute to a more peaceful, prosperous, and equitable world.

16. Conclusion: Navigating the Future of Digital Diplomacy

"The power of digital diplomacy lies in its ability to transcend physical boundaries, reaching people where traditional diplomacy cannot." - Hillary Clinton

As digital technologies continue to reshape the landscape of diplomacy, diplomats and diplomatic institutions find themselves at the intersection of unprecedented opportunities and complex challenges. The concluding chapter serves as a reflection on the transformative journey embarked upon throughout this book, encapsulating the key themes and insights that have emerged. It also serves as a compass pointing towards the future of digital diplomacy, offering strategic guidance for navigating the ever-evolving diplomatic terrain.

In this digital age, diplomats are presented with an array of tools and platforms that have revolutionized the way they engage with global audiences, communicate policy objectives, and navigate international relations. From social media platforms that facilitate real-time dialogue to emerging technologies like artificial intelligence and virtual reality that offer innovative avenues for engagement, the opportunities for diplomatic outreach and influence have expanded exponentially. However, alongside these opportunities come intricate challenges that demand careful consideration and strategic foresight.

As we reflect on the journey through the chapters of this book, several overarching themes emerge. The evolution of digital diplomacy, from its nascent stages to its current state of sophistication, underscores the dynamic nature of diplomatic practice in response to technological advancements. The pivotal role of social media in diplomatic communication highlights the power of digital platforms in shaping public opinion, influencing narratives, and fostering cross-cultural understanding.

Moreover, the integration of emerging technologies such as artificial intelligence, blockchain, and virtual reality signifies a paradigm shift in diplomatic practice, offering diplomats new tools for analysis, decision-making support, and immersive engagement. Yet, this technological revolution brings with it ethical considerations and governance challenges that necessitate careful attention to issues of data privacy, security, and transparency.

Looking ahead, the future of digital diplomacy holds immense promise, but it also presents diplomats and diplomatic institutions with a myriad of strategic imperatives. The need for continuous capacity building and adaptation to technological advancements is paramount, as diplomats must equip themselves with the skills, knowledge, and competencies to navigate the complexities of the digital age. Furthermore, fostering collaboration and diplomatic cooperation, both within and across borders, is essential for addressing global challenges and advancing shared objectives in an interconnected world.

The future of digital diplomacy is characterized by both opportunity and complexity. By embracing technological innovation, upholding ethical standards, and fostering diplomatic collaboration, diplomats can navigate the challenges and seize the opportunities of the digital age, contributing to a more peaceful, prosperous, and sustainable world. As diplomats embark on this journey, they must remain agile, resilient, and forward-thinking, equipped to navigate the evolving diplomatic landscape with integrity and purpose.

16.1 Recap of Key Findings and Insights

Transformation of Diplomacy in the Digital Era: The book outlines how digital technologies have revolutionized diplomatic practice, from traditional modes of communication to innovative digital platforms. Diplomats now have unprecedented opportunities to engage with global audiences, convey policy messages, and shape international narratives through social media, virtual summits, and other digital channels.

The Power of Social Media in Diplomatic Communication: Social media platforms have emerged as potent tools for diplomatic communication, enabling diplomats to conduct public diplomacy, engage in real-time dialogue, and promote cultural exchange. However, the use of social media also raises challenges related to authenticity, credibility, and information overload.

Integration of Emerging Technologies: The book explores the integration of emerging technologies such as artificial intelligence, blockchain, and virtual reality in diplomatic practice. These technologies offer diplomats new avenues for analysis, decision-making support, and immersive communication, but they also raise ethical considerations and governance challenges that require careful attention.

Ethical Considerations and Governance Challenges: As diplomats leverage emerging technologies in digital diplomacy, ethical considerations related to data privacy, security, and transparency become increasingly important. Diplomatic institutions must prioritize ethical governance frameworks to ensure responsible and accountable use of digital technologies in diplomacy.

Capacity Building and Diplomatic Resilience: Diplomatic training and capacity building are essential for equipping diplomats with the skills, knowledge, and competencies to navigate the complexities of digital diplomacy. Diplomatic institutions must invest in digital literacy, cybersecurity training, and technological fluency to empower diplomats to leverage emerging technologies effectively and responsibly.

Collaboration and Diplomatic Cooperation: Collaboration and diplomatic cooperation are crucial for addressing global challenges and advancing shared objectives in the digital age. Diplomats must engage in multilateral dialogue, diplomatic exchanges, and cooperative initiatives to build trust, foster understanding, and forge partnerships in the digital domain.

In summary, the book underscores the transformative impact of digital technologies on diplomatic practice, highlighting both the opportunities and challenges that diplomats face in the digital age. By embracing technological innovation, upholding ethical standards, and fostering diplomatic collaboration, diplomats can navigate the complexities of the digital landscape and contribute to a more peaceful, prosperous, and sustainable world.

16.2 Challenges and Opportunities Ahead in Digital Diplomacy

Challenges:

Cybersecurity Threats: *The increasing reliance on digital platforms exposes diplomatic communications and sensitive information to cybersecurity threats such as hacking, data breaches, and cyber espionage. Diplomatic institutions must invest in robust cybersecurity measures to safeguard against cyber threats and protect the integrity of diplomatic communications.*

Misinformation and Disinformation: *The proliferation of misinformation and disinformation on social media platforms poses a significant challenge to digital diplomacy efforts. Diplomats must navigate the spread of false information, propaganda, and manipulation campaigns that can undermine diplomatic objectives and erode trust in diplomatic institutions.*

Digital Divide: *The digital divide, characterized by disparities in access to technology and digital literacy, hinders inclusive participation in digital diplomacy initiatives. Diplomatic institutions must address inequalities in* *access to technology and ensure that all diplomats have the necessary skills and resources to engage effectively in digital diplomacy efforts.*

Ethical Dilemmas: *The use of emerging technologies such as artificial intelligence and big data in digital diplomacy raises ethical dilemmas related to privacy, bias, and accountability. Diplomatic institutions must navigate these ethical challenges and develop frameworks to ensure responsible and ethical use of technology in diplomacy.*

Geopolitical Tensions: *Geopolitical tensions and rivalries in the digital domain can impede diplomatic cooperation and collaboration. Diplomats must navigate complex geopolitical dynamics and work towards building trust, fostering dialogue, and finding common ground with other states and stakeholders in the digital arena.*

Opportunities:

Enhanced Connectivity: *Digital technologies offer diplomats unprecedented opportunities to connect with global audiences, engage in real-time dialogue, and foster cross-cultural understanding. Diplomatic institutions can leverage digital platforms to expand their reach, amplify their messages, and build digital bridges between nations.*

Innovative Diplomatic Tools: *Emerging technologies such as artificial intelligence, blockchain, and virtual reality offer diplomats innovative tools for analysis, decision-making support, and immersive communication. Diplomatic institutions can harness these technologies to enhance diplomatic agility, resilience, and effectiveness in navigating complex global challenges.*

Public Diplomacy and Cultural Exchange: *Social media platforms provide diplomats with powerful tools for conducting public diplomacy and promoting cultural exchange. Diplomatic institutions can leverage social media to showcase their country's culture, values, and diplomatic* *initiatives, fostering mutual understanding and strengthening diplomatic ties with foreign audiences.*

Multilateral Collaboration: *Digital diplomacy enables diplomats to engage in multilateral dialogue, diplomatic exchanges, and cooperative initiatives with other states and international organizations. Diplomatic institutions can leverage digital platforms to foster collaboration, build consensus, and address global challenges such as climate change, cybersecurity, and public health.*

Capacity Building and Diplomatic Innovation: *Diplomatic training and capacity building are essential for equipping diplomats with the skills, knowledge, and competencies to navigate the complexities of digital diplomacy. Diplomatic institutions can invest in digital literacy programs, cybersecurity training, and technological fluency to empower diplomats to leverage emerging technologies effectively and responsibly.*

In conclusion, while digital diplomacy presents a range of challenges, it also offers diplomats unprecedented opportunities to enhance connectivity, foster collaboration, and advance diplomatic objectives in the digital age. By addressing the challenges and leveraging the opportunities of digital diplomacy, diplomats can navigate the complexities of the digital landscape and contribute to a more peaceful, prosperous, and sustainable world.

16.3 Recommendations for Policymakers, Diplomats, and Practitioners

Some recommendations for policymakers, diplomats, and practitioners in the field of digital diplomacy:

Policymakers:

Develop Comprehensive Cybersecurity Policies: *Policymakers should prioritize the development of comprehensive cybersecurity policies to safeguard diplomatic communications and sensitive information against cyber threats. This includes investing in robust cybersecurity infrastructure, conducting regular security audits, and implementing best practices for data protection.*

Promote Digital Literacy and Training Programs: *Policymakers should support initiatives aimed at promoting digital literacy and providing training programs for diplomats and foreign service professionals. This includes offering courses on cybersecurity, emerging technologies, and digital communication strategies to equip diplomats with the necessary skills and knowledge to navigate the digital landscape effectively.*

Foster Multilateral Cooperation: *Policymakers should prioritize diplomatic cooperation and collaboration at the international level to address common challenges in the digital domain. This includes fostering dialogue, sharing best practices, and establishing norms and standards for responsible conduct in cyberspace.*

Address the Digital Divide: *Policymakers should work to address inequalities in access to technology and digital literacy to ensure inclusive participation in digital diplomacy initiatives. This may involve investing in infrastructure development, providing access to affordable internet services, and offering training programs for underserved populations.*

Promote Ethical and Responsible Use of Technology: *Policymakers should promote ethical and responsible use of technology in diplomacy by establishing guidelines and frameworks to govern the use of emerging technologies such as artificial intelligence, blockchain, and virtual reality.*

This includes addressing ethical dilemmas related to privacy, bias, and accountability in the digital domain.

Diplomats:

Stay Updated on Emerging Technologies: *Diplomats should stay informed about emerging technologies and their potential impact on diplomatic practice. This includes attending training programs, workshops, and conferences on digital diplomacy and emerging technologies to enhance their technological literacy and awareness.*

Engage in Continuous Learning and Skill Development: *Diplomats should engage in continuous learning and skill development to adapt to the evolving digital landscape. This may involve participating in online courses, workshops, and seminars on digital communication strategies, cybersecurity, and data analytics.*

Leverage Digital Platforms for Engagement: *Diplomats should leverage digital platforms such as social media, virtual summits, and online forums to engage with global audiences, convey policy messages, and promote cultural exchange. This includes maintaining active social media profiles, participating in digital diplomacy initiatives, and fostering dialogue with foreign counterparts.*

Adhere to Ethical Standards: *Diplomats should adhere to ethical standards and guidelines governing the use of digital technologies in diplomacy. This includes respecting privacy rights, avoiding the spread of misinformation, and upholding diplomatic integrity and professionalism in online interactions.*

Collaborate with Stakeholders: *Diplomats should collaborate with stakeholders from other government agencies, international organizations, civil society, and the private sector to address common challenges and advance shared objectives in the digital domain. This* *includes fostering partnerships, sharing best practices, and coordinating efforts to promote digital diplomacy initiatives.*

Practitioners:

Develop Digital Communication Strategies: *Practitioners in the field of digital diplomacy should develop comprehensive digital communication strategies to effectively convey policy messages, engage with audiences, and promote diplomatic objectives online. This includes identifying target audiences, crafting compelling content, and leveraging digital platforms to reach diverse stakeholders.*

Monitor and Analyze Digital Trends: *Practitioners should monitor and analyze digital trends and developments to stay ahead of emerging issues and opportunities in the digital domain. This includes conducting social media listening, sentiment analysis, and data analytics to understand public opinion, track online conversations, and inform diplomatic decision-making.*

Build Digital Resilience: *Practitioners should build digital resilience to mitigate risks and respond effectively to cybersecurity threats, misinformation campaigns, and other digital challenges. This includes implementing security measures, conducting crisis simulations, and developing contingency plans to protect diplomatic communications and assets.*

Engage in Digital Diplomacy Initiatives: *Practitioners should actively engage in digital diplomacy initiatives and collaborative projects to leverage the power of digital technologies for diplomatic purposes. This includes participating in virtual summits, online forums, and cultural exchange programs to foster dialogue, build relationships, and advance diplomatic objectives in the digital age.*

Promote Digital Diplomacy Best Practices: *Practitioners should promote digital diplomacy best practices and share lessons learned with colleagues and peers across the diplomatic community. This includes organizing workshops, webinars, and knowledge-sharing events to exchange ideas, showcase success stories, and foster innovation in digital diplomacy practice.*

By implementing these recommendations, policymakers, diplomats, and practitioners can enhance the effectiveness and impact of digital diplomacy initiatives, navigate the complexities of the digital landscape, and contribute to a more peaceful, prosperous, and sustainable world.

16.4 Envisioning the Future Landscape of Digital Diplomacy

The future landscape of digital diplomacy promises to be dynamic, interconnected, and transformative, driven by rapid advancements in technology and evolving geopolitical dynamics. As we look ahead, several key trends and developments are likely to shape the practice of digital diplomacy:

- **Integration of Emerging Technologies**

Emerging technologies such as artificial intelligence, blockchain, and augmented reality will continue to play a pivotal role in digital diplomacy, offering diplomats new tools and platforms for analysis, communication, and engagement. AI-driven predictive analytics, blockchain-based diplomatic agreements, and immersive AR/VR experiences will become increasingly prevalent in diplomatic practice, enhancing diplomats' capabilities and effectiveness in navigating complex global challenges.

- **Enhanced Data Analytics and Predictive Insights:**

Diplomatic institutions will leverage advanced data analytics and predictive insights to inform decision-making, anticipate emerging trends, and assess the impact of diplomatic initiatives. Big data analytics, sentiment analysis, and social media listening tools will enable diplomats to gain deeper insights into public opinion, track geopolitical developments, and tailor their communication strategies to effectively engage with diverse audiences.

- **Virtual Diplomatic Gatherings and Conferences:**

Virtual summits, conferences, and diplomatic gatherings will become more commonplace in the future, offering diplomats innovative platforms for dialogue, collaboration, and diplomacy. Virtual reality technologies will enable diplomats to participate in immersive diplomatic experiences, engage in virtual negotiations, and conduct high-level meetings without the constraints of physical location, fostering greater inclusivity and accessibility in diplomatic engagements.

- **Diplomatic Cooperation in Cyberspace:**

Diplomatic cooperation in cyberspace will become increasingly important as states grapple with cybersecurity threats, disinformation campaigns, and other digital challenges. Diplomatic institutions will work together to establish norms, rules, and cooperative mechanisms to enhance cybersecurity, combat cyber threats, and promote responsible behavior in cyberspace, fostering trust and stability in the digital domain.

- **Citizen Diplomacy and Digital Activism**

Citizen diplomacy and digital activism will play a significant role in shaping international relations, as empowered individuals and non-state actors leverage digital platforms to advocate for social change, promote human rights, and hold governments accountable. Diplomats will need to engage with digital activists, civil society organizations, and grassroots movements to address emerging issues, amplify marginalized voices, and build partnerships for positive change.

- **Ethical Governance and Digital Diplomacy Principles**

Ethical governance and adherence to digital diplomacy principles will be critical for maintaining trust, transparency, and accountability in diplomatic practice. Diplomatic institutions will develop frameworks and guidelines to govern the responsible and ethical use of technology in diplomacy, addressing issues such as data privacy, algorithmic bias, and digital rights to ensure that digital diplomacy remains aligned with diplomatic values and principles.

In conclusion, the future landscape of digital diplomacy holds immense promise for shaping a more connected, collaborative, and resilient international community. By embracing emerging technologies, fostering diplomatic cooperation, and upholding ethical standards, diplomats can navigate the complexities of the digital age and leverage the power of digital diplomacy to address global challenges, promote peace, and advance shared prosperity in the 21st century.

Bibliography

Books

Acs, Z. J., & Audretsch, D. B. (2010). Entrepreneurship and economic development: The role of entrepreneurship in the new economy. Routledge.

Afrin, L. B., Rahman, M. S., & Chowdhury, S. F. (2020). Telemedicine and digital health services: A rising movement during the COVID-19 pandemic in Bangladesh. Heliyon, 6(11), e05490.

Aroca, P., & Stalker, P. (2015). Global mobility regimes. Springer.

Aronoff, J., & Orrenius, P. (2016). Diaspora, development, and democracy: The domestic impact of international migration from India. Oxford University Press.

Baldwin, K. (2020). Virtual Reality and Augmented Reality in Diplomacy. Oxford Research Encyclopedia of International Studies. doi:10.1093/acrefore/9780190846626.013.1097

Bates, C., Brown, T., & Hainsworth, S. (2003). Technology, gender, and power in Africa. Nordic Africa Institute.

Bauböck, R., & Faist, T. (2010). Diaspora and transnationalism: Concepts, theories and methods. Amsterdam University Press.

Bauböck, R., & Smith, M. P. (2017). Citizenship policies for an age of migration. Oxford University Press.

Bjola, C., & Holmes, M. (2015). Digital Diplomacy: Theory and Practice. New York, NY: Routledge.

Bjola, C., & Pamment, J. (2018). Countering disinformation: The quest for a global response. Oxford University Press.

Bodansky, D. (2016). The Paris climate change agreement: A new hope? American Journal of International Law, 110(2), 288-319.

Bryant, R. L., & Holt, M. (Eds.). (2020). Diplomacy in the Digital Age. Brill.

Cairney, P., & Yamamoto, T. (2019). Digital Diplomacy: Theory and Practice. New York, NY: Routledge.

Carpenter, C. (2016). Digital diplomacy: Statecraft in the cyber age. Lynne Rienner Publishers.

Cashore, B., Auld, G., & Newsom, D. (2004). Governing through markets: Forest certification and the emergence of non-state authority. Yale University Press.

Chen, Y. (2019). Digital Governance: New Governance Model for a Digital Age. In Proceedings of the 22nd Annual International Conference on Digital Government Research (pp. 177-182). ACM.

Choudhury, M. M., et al. (2020). Virtual Diplomacy: The Future of International Relations. London, UK: Routledge.

Cull, N. J. (2019). Public Diplomacy: Foundations for Global Engagement in the Digital Age. Cambridge, UK: Polity Press.

DeNardis, L. (2020). The Global War for Internet Governance. New Haven, CT: Yale University Press.

Falkner, R. (2016). The Paris Agreement and the new logic of international climate politics. International Affairs, 92(5), 1107-1125.

Fischer, J., et al. (2022). Digital Diplomacy: Theory and Practice in the Digital Era. New York, NY: Oxford University Press.

Fisher, A. (2017). Digital Diplomacy: A History. Montreal: McGill-Queen's University Press.

Fisher, E. (2021). The Rise of Artificial Intelligence in Diplomacy. The Diplomat. Retrieved from https://thediplomat.com/2021/03/the-rise-of-artificial-intelligence-in-diplomacy/

Fricker, H. A., Liebmann, B., Roberts, J. B., & Jones, P. D. (2020). Benchmarking global space-based climate reanalyses using radiosonde temperature and geopotential height data. Quarterly Journal of the Royal Meteorological Society, 146(731), 2209-2233.

Gamlen, A. (2008). The emigration state and the modern geopolitical imagination. Political Geography, 27(8), 840-856.

Gamlen, A. (2014). Diaspora engagement policies: What are they, and what kinds of states use them? International Migration Review, 48(3), 577-611.

Gilboa, E. (2016). Digital Diplomacy: Theory and Practice. New York, NY: Routledge.

Gilboa, E. (2018). Digital Diplomacy: The Impact of the Internet on International Relations. London: Rowman & Littlefield.

Gleick, P. H. (2010). Bottled and sold: The story behind our obsession with bottled water. Island Press.

Hafkin, N., & Huyer, S. (Eds.). (2006). Cinderella or cyberella? Empowering women in the knowledge society. Kumarian Press.

Hocking, B., & Melissen, J. (Eds.). (2015). New diplomacy in the information age: A study of information management in the conduct of diplomacy. Brill.

Hoffman, A. J. (2017). Climate governance at the crossroads: Experimenting with a global response after Kyoto. Oxford University Press.

Hoffmann, M. (2018). The Ethics of Cultural Diplomacy. Oxford, UK: Oxford University Press.

Jakhu, R., & Pelton, J. N. (2018). Routledge handbook of space law. Routledge.

Johnson-Freese, J. (2018). Space as a strategic asset. Columbia University Press.

Johnson-Freese, J. (2020). Security in space: The next generation. Routledge.

Johnson-Freese, J. (2021). Addressing the security impacts of proliferating megaconstellations. Space Policy, 56, 101608.

Kerr, P. (2019). Digital Diplomacy and International Security: The Challenges and Opportunities of the Internet. New York, NY: Routledge.

Kotliar, O., et al. (2021). The Impact of Virtual Diplomacy on Decision-Making Processes. International Studies Perspectives, 22(4), 401-420.

Kreuter, M. W., Lukwago, S. N., Bucholtz, R. D., Clark, E. M., & Sanders-Thompson, V. (2000). Achieving cultural appropriateness in health promotion programs: Targeted and tailored approaches. Health Education & Behavior, 27(2), 133-146.

Kurbalija, J. (2018). An introduction to internet governance. DiploFoundation.

Kurbalija, J., & Katrandjiev, H. (2018). Diplomacy in the age of artificial intelligence. DiploFoundation.

Logsdon, J. M. (2015). After Apollo? Richard Nixon and the American space program. Palgrave Macmillan.

Manor, I. (2017). Digital Diplomacy: Theory and Practice. New York, NY: Routledge.

Manor, I. (2019). The Digitalization of Public Diplomacy. New York, NY: Palgrave Macmillan.

Mayer-Schönberger, V., & Cukier, K. (2013). Big data: A revolution that will transform how we live, work, and think. Houghton Mifflin Harcourt.

Meier, P. (2015). Digital Humanitarians: How Big Data Is Changing the Face of Humanitarian Response. Boca Raton, FL: CRC Press.

Merlingen, M., & Ojanen, H. (Eds.). (2020). Artificial intelligence and digital diplomacy. Brill.

Muller, D. C. (2020). Digital Diplomacy: Conversations on Innovation in Foreign Policy. New York, NY: Oxford University Press.

Nasiri, M. (2019). Blockchain technology and diplomatic communication. Diplomacy & Statecraft, 30(1), 18-38.

Novillo-Ortiz, D., Dumit, E., & Dzenowagis, J. (2015). eHealth in Latin America and the Caribbean: Development and policy issues. Pan American Health Organization.

Nye, J. S. (2019). The Future of Power. New York, NY: PublicAffairs.

Nye, J. S. (2021). Do Cyber Norms Matter? Cyber Norms as Confidence-Building Measures. Foreign Policy Analysis, 17(2), 249-257.

Paris Peace Forum. (n.d.). Paris Peace Forum. Retrieved from https://parispeaceforum.org/

Pascal, S., & Slobodchikoff, M. (2020). Virtual Diplomacy: How Technology Changes Diplomacy. New York, NY: Springer.

Riordan, S. (2020). Virtual Cultural Diplomacy: Engaging Audiences during the COVID-19 Pandemic. Journal of Cultural Management and Policy, 9(2), 171-186.

Schmitt, M. N. (2017). Tallinn Manual 2.0 on the International Law Applicable to Cyber Operations. Cambridge, UK: Cambridge University Press.

Sevin, E., & Ba, C. (2018). Digital diplomacy: An exploration of theory and practice. New Perspectives on Turkey, 58, 161-185.

Shaikh, A. (2019). Diplomatic innovation: The next frontier for diplomacy. Diplomatic Courier.

Singh, K. (2021). India's Vaccine Diplomacy: A Global Nudge Strategy in Times of Pandemic. In A. Saikia (Ed.), The Politics of Vaccination: A Global Perspective (pp. 125-141). Cham: Springer.

Smith, J. (2020). Digital trade agreements: Implications for global commerce. Cambridge University Press.

Smith, J. (2020). Tweeting for trade: The use of Twitter in economic diplomacy. Digital Diplomacy Review, 4(1), 45-58.

Stanger, A. (2019). The Hacker and the State: Cyber Attacks and the New Normal of Geopolitics. New York, NY: Oxford University Press.

Stares, P. B. (2019). Space and international politics: A global perspective. Routledge.

Tikk, E., & Russell, C. (2020). Cyber Norms and International Security: From Conceptual History to Practice. New York, NY: Oxford University Press.

Weldes, J. (2015). Globalization and the Production of Diplomatic Culture. In H. Neumann, & A. Gstöhl (Eds.), Diplomatic Cultures and International Politics: Translations, Spaces and Alternatives (pp. 21-38). New York, NY: Routledge.

Zwitter, A. (2019). Environmental security and digital diplomacy. In Handbook on the international political economy of security (pp. 411-429). Edward Elgar Publishing.

Articles

Adger, W. N., Arnell, N. W., & Tompkins, E. L. (2009). Successful adaptation to climate change across scales. Global Environmental Change, 15(2), 77-86.

Agarwal, S., Perry, H. B., Long, L. A., & Labrique, A. B. (2020). Evidence on feasibility and effective use of mHealth strategies by frontline health workers in developing countries: Systematic review. Tropical Medicine & International Health, 25(4), 412-424.

Albinger, E. J. (2020). Space resources governance: Comparing practices and prospects in the United States and Luxembourg. Acta Astronautica, 167, 110-118.

Barbier, E. B., & Burgess, J. C. (2017). The sustainable development goals and the systems approach to sustainability. Economics: The Open-Access, Open-Assessment E-Journal, 11(2017-26), 1-15.

Barthold, C., & Kunz, M. (2019). Methodological challenges in space-related innovation studies. Space Policy, 50, 101345.

Barua, R. (2017). Innovation in space activities: Evolution of organizational and institutional frameworks. Space Policy, 42, 48-54.

Biermann, F., & Boas, I. (2010). Preparing for a warmer world: Towards a global governance system to protect climate refugees. Global Environmental Politics, 10(1), 60-88.

Blöbaum, B., & Hossain, M. (2020). Norms and values in global environmental communication: A multi-method study of determinants and consequences of the news audience's environmental consciousness. Environmental Communication, 14(5), 646-660.

Bose, P. K., & Pervin, F. (2019). MHealth for COVID-19: A perspective from Bangladesh. Health Policy and Technology, 9(4), 368-372.

Brannen, J., & Patrick, H. (2017). Mixed methods research. In The SAGE handbook of qualitative research (pp. 564-574). Sage Publications.

Braun, V., & Clarke, V. (2019). Reflecting on reflexive thematic analysis. Qualitative Research in Sport, Exercise and Health, 11(4), 589-597.

Brooks, S. K., Webster, R. K., Smith, L. E., Woodland, L., Wessely, S., Greenberg, N., & Rubin, G. J. (2020). The psychological impact of quarantine and how to reduce it: Rapid review of the evidence. The Lancet, 395(10227), 912-920.

Cachia, R., Sterkens, P., & Korte, W. B. (2020). The state of European digital diplomacy in 2020: A country-by-country analysis. Digital Diplomacy Review, 4(1), 59-74.

Chen, T., Dwyer, L., & Firth, T. (2020). Climate change communication in tourism: A systematic literature review. Journal of Sustainable Tourism, 28(10), 1477-1496.

Chen, Y. (2019). Digital Governance: New Governance Model for a Digital Age. In Proceedings of the 22nd Annual International Conference on Digital Government Research (pp. 177-182). ACM.

Choy, E. S., & Chen, K. H. (2018). Exploring the determinants of public diplomacy effectiveness. Place Branding and Public Diplomacy, 14(3), 167-179.

Costello, A., Abbas, M., Allen, A., Ball, S., Bell, S., Bellamy, R., ... & Zaidi, A. K. M. (2009). Managing the health effects of climate change. The Lancet, 373(9676), 1693-1733.

Datta, S. (2020). Climate change communication through social media: A study on Twitter conversations about climate change during the COP24. Environmental Communication, 14(1), 110-125.

Davies, T., & Jenkins, A. (2013). The Rise of the Digital Humanitarian. Foreign Affairs, 92(6), 45-54.

de Leeuw, A., & Valois, P. (2019). The global governance of geoengineering: The role of science advisors in creating institutional frameworks. Science and Public Policy, 46(6), 934-944.

De Sousa, M. J., Correia, A., & Ribeiro, P. (2018). News coverage of climate change: An exploratory study of determinants and constraints. Environmental Communication, 12(5), 593-608.

Diekmann, A., Jann, B., & Przepiorka, W. (2020). A general strategy for analyzing causality in time-series cross-section data. Sociological Methods & Research, 49(3), 519-547.

Dodds, K., & Strauss, S. (2019). Data assemblages in climate change communication: Investigating the circulation and effects of climate data. Environmental Communication, 13(5), 624-638.

Dryzek, J. S., Downes, D., Hunold, C., Schlosberg, D., & Hernes, H. K. (2019). Greening global democracy. Cambridge University Press.

Duarte, R., & Pinho, A. P. (2018). An overview of Portugal's digital diplomacy 2.0. Digital Diplomacy Review, 4(1), 75-92.

Engle Merry, S. (2016). Sedimented stories: Law and the construction of human rights. American Journal of Sociology, 122(1), 1-51.

Evensen, D., & Leiby, J. (2020). The evolving role of space actors: Toward space traffic management. Space Policy, 50, 101352.

Flecha, R., Soler, M., & Sordé, T. (2015). Social impact of intergroup contact: A sociological survey of the Catalan case. Social Science Research, 52, 523-538.

Fleurbaey, M., & Gajdos, T. (2010). A common currency for the assessment of inequality: The equivalent income of EU citizens. Social Choice and Welfare, 35(2), 231-253.

Fortson, L. F. (2015). Editorial: Recent progress in literacy research. Journal of Research in Reading, 38(3), 247-253.

Fox, M. F. (2005). Gender, family characteristics, and publication productivity among scientists. Social Studies of Science, 35(1), 131-150.

Frank, D. J., & Meyer, J. W. (2007). University expansion and the knowledge society. Theory and Society, 36(4), 287-311.

Fröhlich, X., & Entman, R. M. (2020). Predicting agenda-setting effects: Interaction among audience interest, media coverage, and media credibility. Journal of Communication, 70(4), 525-545.

Garsten, C. (2010). On science and democracy: Expertise, accountability, and deliberation in global governance. Global Governance, 16(1), 89-105.

Gerber, A. S., Karlan, D., & Bergan, D. (2009). Does the media matter? A field experiment measuring the effect of newspapers on voting behavior and political opinions. American Economic Journal: Applied Economics, 1(2), 35-52.

Ghatak, S., & Stefanou, S. E. (2017). Factor demands, cost curves, and supply chain organization in space: Panel data evidence from the International Space Station. Journal of Productivity Analysis, 47(2), 171-185.

Giles, M. W., & Hertz, D. B. (2017). Rethinking the politics of space. Space Policy, 41, 45-51.

Glaeser, E. L., & Sunstein, C. R. (2014). Why does balanced news produce unbalanced views? National Bureau of Economic Research. https://doi.org/10.3386/w19858

Gokhale, N., & Kandlikar, M. (2020). Climate science needs to change its language. Nature Climate Change, 10(1), 12-14.

Gong, X., Shen, X., & Guo, J. (2018). Toward global climate justice? Analyzing China's role in international climate negotiations. Journal of Environmental Studies and Sciences, 8(3), 337-345.

Graells-Garrido, E., & Lalmas, M. (2019). #LifeOrientation: Exploring the potential of Instagram hashtags to support identity transition after breast cancer. Journal of the Association for Information Science and Technology, 70(4), 309-320.

Green, J., & Thorogood, N. (2004). Qualitative methods for health research. Sage.

Grossman, G., Humphreys, M., & Sacramone-Lutz, G. (2018). Civil war, social networks, and the spread of Ebola in Liberia. Journal of Development Economics, 134, 161-175.

Haas, P. M. (2018). Introduction: Epistemic communities and epistemes in global climate change governance. In The Oxford Handbook of

Comparative Environmental Politics (pp. 1-30). Oxford University Press.

Hagberg, L., Höglund, K., & Wagnsson, C. (2019). Military and civil space policies: A comparison of European, Asian and American perspectives. Space Policy, 49, 31-36.

Hart, P. S., & Nisbet, E. C. (2012). Boomerang effects in science communication: How motivated reasoning and identity cues amplify opinion polarization about climate mitigation policies. Communication Research, 39(6), 701-723.

Hastie, R., & Dawes, R. M. (2010). Rational choice in an uncertain world: The psychology of judgment and decision making. Sage.

Hayden, C. (2018). The Role of Social Media in Public Diplomacy: An Analysis of the US Embassies on Facebook. Journal of Political Marketing, 17(4), 383-404.

Hennig, J. (2019). The role of social media in global digital diplomacy. Digital Diplomacy Review, 1(1), 31-42.

Herrmann, R. K., & Fischerkeller, M. P. (2015). Beyond the public sphere: Opinions, attitudes, and perception in space policy making. Space Policy, 34, 29-38.

Hisschemöller, M., & Hoppe, R. (1995). Coping with intractable controversies: The case for problem structuring in policy design and analysis. Knowledge and Policy, 8(4), 40-60.

Ho, C. M. F., Lai, G., Leung, J. M. Y., & Leung, M. M. (2020). Understanding the psychological impact of the COVID-19 pandemic on digital diplomacy: Preliminary analysis of Twitter data. Digital Diplomacy Review, 3(1), 91-111.

Hoggan, J. (2009). I'm right and you're an idiot: The toxic state of public discourse and how to clean it up. New Society Publishers.

Holgate, S. T. (2017). Climate change and health: An international perspective. Yearbook of Medical Informatics, 26(1), 6-8.

Hölscher, L., & Wittje, R. (2017). Reaching for the stars: India's ever-closer grasp of space power. Journal of Strategic Studies, 40(6), 773-805.

Hoppe, R., van der Knaap, P., Koppenjan, J., & Pregernig, M. (2010). A management perspective on policy networks. Policy Studies Journal, 38(1), 169-171.

Houghton, J. (2019). Global warming: The complete briefing. Cambridge University Press.

Howell, S. E., & Susskind, L. E. (2001). Bringing stakeholders into community-based risk assessment: Tools and techniques. Risk Analysis, 21(4), 681-702.

Hudson, S., & Thalhammer, E. (2020). Social Media and Crisis Communication in Diplomacy: A Case Study of the U.S. State Department's Response to the Nepal Earthquake. Public Relations Review, 46(3), 101829.

Hwang, H. M., & Han, J. H. (2018). Public diplomacy 2.0 in South Korea: A quantitative content analysis of the Facebook and Twitter channels of the South Korean embassy in the United States. Place Branding and Public Diplomacy, 14(1), 1-17.

Ilyushin, L. S., & Yatchmenyova, Y. V. (2017). Climate change coverage by international and national media in Russia: Political determinants and framing characteristics. Environmental Communication, 11(6), 784-801.

Islam, M. N. (2018). Climate diplomacy: A study of Bangladesh's strategic engagements. Asian Affairs, 39(1), 22-42.

Jang, S. M., Mckeever, B. W., & St Louis, C. (2019). Social media, hashtags, and content moderation: A network analysis of #MyNYPD tweets. Social Media + Society, 5(3), 1-12.

Jasanoff, S. (2010). A new climate for society. Theory, Culture & Society, 27(2-3), 233-253.

Jensen, B. (2017). Digital Diplomacy in Practice: Swedish Embassies on Facebook. The Hague Journal of Diplomacy, 12(3), 343-368.

Juhola, S., & Westerhoff, L. (2011). Challenges of adaptation to climate change across multiple scales: A case study of network governance in two European countries. Environmental Science & Policy, 14(3), 239-247.

Khan, M. (2019). The Impact of Social Media on Diplomacy: A Critical Review. International Studies, 56(2), 181-198.

Kim, H., Lee, K., & Jung, J. (2016). Theorizing diplomatic relations on Twitter: A comparative analysis of South Korea and Japan. The Hague Journal of Diplomacy, 11(1), 67-87.

Kivistö, S., & Ylä-Anttila, T. (2019). Power asymmetry in digital diplomacy: The case of US embassies in Twitter. Place Branding and Public Diplomacy, 15(4), 230-245.

Kollmuss, A., & Agyeman, J. (2002). Mind the gap: Why do people act environmentally and what are the barriers to pro-environmental behavior? Environmental Education Research, 8(3), 239-260.

Kondoh, T. (2018). Strategic narratives in the Japan-US alliance: The utility of narratives in security studies. Contemporary Security Policy, 39(3), 345-366.

Krueger, R. A., & Casey, M. A. (2015). Focus groups: A practical guide for applied research. Sage publications.

Lachapelle, E., & Patenaude, G. (2016). Climate change adaptation: From resilience to transformation. Routledge.

Lall, U., & Deichmann, U. (2012). Density and disasters: Economics of urban hazard risk. In Urbanization and sustainability (pp. 185-210). Springer.

Lefsrud, L. M., & Meyer, R. E. (2012). Science or science fiction? Professionals' discursive construction of climate change. Organization Studies, 33(11), 1477-1506.

LeMay, M., & Lönnqvist, H. (2017). The new field of space law: Challenges and opportunities. Space Policy, 39, 9-14.

Levallet, N., & Trappmann, M. (2018). Organizing stakeholder consultations: Can the facilitator role be operationalized? Public Management Review, 20(1), 64-84.

Li, S. X., & Rourke, M. (2018). When do citizens follow the twitter feeds of embassies? Examining the influence of online diplomacy activities on citizens' issue attention. Foreign Policy Analysis, 14(4), 483-502.

Linturi, R., & Mukhtar, A. (2020). Adoption and development of telemedicine in Kenya: A case study of the Kenyan Health System. In Exploring telemedicine: Devices, clinical applications, and emerging trends (pp. 1-26). IGI Global.

Lohmann, L. (2012). Uncertainty markets and carbon markets: Varieties of capitalism in climate change policy. New Political Economy, 17(5), 603-625.

Lopez-Arellano, M., & Marsden, S. V. (2015). Climate change and the security and stability of the Arctic region. The Journal of Strategic Studies, 38(1-2), 98-126.

Lopez-Tarruella, A. (2021). Challenges and Opportunities of Virtual Diplomacy: A Case Study of the United Nations General Assembly. Journal of Diplomatic Studies, 20(3), 321-338.

Lu, Y., Zhang, L., Wang, F., & Ding, Y. (2020). The role of digital diplomacy in crisis communication: A case study of China's responses to the MH370 incident. Digital Diplomacy Review, 4(1), 93-108.

Mair, J., & Martens, K. (2005). Politicizing Europe: Integration and mass politics. Rowman & Littlefield.

Mannion, R., Exworthy, M., Powell, M., & Davies, H. T. O. (2009). Learning from failure? The politics of trust and organizational performance. Journal of Health Services Research & Policy, 14(2), 78-82.

Marchetti, R., & Alvarado, M. (2018). Analyzing international space cooperation through national space policies. Space Policy, 43, 67-76.

McAdams, D. P., & Olson, B. D. (2010). Personality development: Continuity and change over the life course. Annual Review of Psychology, 61, 517-542.

Mialon, M., & Mialon, J. (2019). Corporate political activity and health: A systematic literature review. Journal of Public Health Policy, 40(1), 75-94.

Moos, M. (2019). Climate change communication and the media. In Handbook of climate change communication: Vol. 3. Case studies in climate change communication (pp. 45-55). Springer.

Moss, T. (2016). Climate change and social movements. In The Oxford handbook of social movements (pp. 287-304). Oxford University Press.

Mutz, D. C. (2006). How the mass media divide us. In R. Shapiro & L. Jacobs (Eds.), The Oxford Handbook of American Public Opinion and the Media (pp. 186-209). Oxford University Press.

Newig, J., Schulz, D., Jahn, T., & Basse, E. M. (2016). Disentangling puzzles of spatial scales and participation in environmental governance—The case of governance re-scaling through the European Water Framework Directive. Environmental Management, 58(6), 998-1014.

Nielsen, R. K. (2018). Making news: The role of social media in news consumption and news attitudes in the Nordic countries. Digital Journalism, 6(3), 343-363.

Norris, P. (2000). A virtuous circle: Political communications in postindustrial societies. Cambridge University Press.

O'Neill, S. J., & Nicholson-Cole, S. (2009). "Fear won't do it": Promoting positive engagement with climate change through visual and iconic representations. Science Communication, 30(3), 355-379.

O'Neill, S. J., Boykoff, M., & Niemeyer, S. (2013). Communicating climate change: Conduits, content, and consensus. Wiley Interdisciplinary Reviews: Climate Change, 4(5), 367-376.

O'Neill, S. J., Williams, H. T., Kurz, T., Wiersma, B., & Boykoff, M. (2015). Dominant frames in legacy and social media coverage of the IPCC Fifth Assessment Report. Nature Climate Change, 5(4), 380-385.

Oklobdzija, S. (2019). Social Media and Diplomacy: A Study of the Swedish Foreign Ministry's Digital Diplomacy Campaigns. International Studies Perspectives, 20(4), 365-383.

Olsen, M. E. (2020). From rules of the game to an arena of competition: Environmental inter-state relations in the twenty-first century. International Environmental Agreements: Politics, Law and Economics, 20(3), 325-345.

Orszag, J. M., & Orszag, P. R. (2019). Technological change and growth in health care spending. Journal of Economic Perspectives, 33(4), 95-112.

Osnes, E. (2012). Changing the atmosphere: Expert knowledge and environmental governance. The MIT Press.

Pádua, J. A., & Bueno, P. R. (2018). National and transnational policy entrepreneurs: Brazil and the global environmental agenda. Review of International Studies, 44(5), 813-834.

Paquin, J. (2010). Multilateralizing climate change: An alternative strategy. Global Environmental Politics, 10(2), 16-21.

Pauwelyn, J. (2007). Conflict of norms in public international law: How WTO law relates to other rules of international law. Cambridge University Press.

Pegram, T., & Haddou, M. (2018). A space policy for Africa: Strategic, policy and regulatory perspectives. African Futures Paper, 15.

Pérez de Armiño, K., & Kurbalija, J. (2019). A digital revolution: A modern diplomacy by design. Global Affairs, 5(2-3), 245-253.

Persha, L., Andersson, K. P., & Olsson, L. (2017). Why resilience is unappealing to social science: Theoretical and empirical investigations of the scientific use of resilience. Science Advances, 3(5), e1700670.

Petley, D. N., Hearn, G. J., Hart, A., Rosser, N. J., & Dunning, S. A. (2007). Trends in landslide occurrence in Nepal. Natural Hazards, 43(1), 23-44.

Phillips, T. (2017). Weather matters: Presenting uncertainty in public weather reports. Public Understanding of Science, 26(4), 414-427.

Pietrzyk-Kaszyńska, A., & Nowak, P. (2020). Innovation in space companies: A review of major trends and methods. Space Policy, 50, 101347.

Plass, D., & Lövbrand, E. (2020). The politics of meaning-making in climate governance: The case of Swedish forest politics. Global Environmental Politics, 20(3), 56-74.

Pralle, S. B. (2006). Branching out, digging in: Environmental advocacy and agenda setting. Georgetown University Press.

Przeszlowska, A. (2020). How climate change is covered in Polish media: A quantitative analysis. Environmental Communication, 14(2), 191-203.

Quist, L. M., & Röling, N. (2010). Cocreating sustainable urban futures: A primer on applying transition management in cities. Springer.

Rayner, S. (2010). How to eat an elephant: A bottom-up approach to climate policy. Climate Policy, 10(6), 615-621.

Reckwitz, A. (2002). Toward a theory of social practices: A development in culturalist theorizing. European Journal of Social Theory, 5(2), 243-263.

Reddy, M. V. (2018). The dynamics of India's space power. The Journal of Strategic Studies, 41(5-6), 887-918.

Rehmann, L. (2018). The global risks of the Belt and Road Initiative. The International Spectator, 53(2), 116-130.

Reis, L. S. (2020). Global and local climate governance: Shifting roles and capacity building needs. Environmental Policy and Governance, 30(5), 307-316.

Rhodes, R. A. W. (1996). The new governance: Governing without government. Political Studies, 44(4), 652-667.

Ricciardi, L., & Losavio, G. (2017). The geo-strategic importance of the Arctic in the 21st century. Geopolitics, History, and International Relations, 9(1), 125-138.

Ricciardi, L., & Losavio, G. (2019). The geopolitics of climate change and the role of the Arctic. Geopolitics, 24(1), 130-145.

Rojas-López, M., & Barros, J. F. (2018). Bridging digital divides in times of disaster: Explaining the speed of Internet recovery after Hurricane Maria. Telematics and Informatics, 35(6), 1626-1640.

Rossini, P. M. M. (2020). Small satellites and their impact on space sustainability. Space Policy, 50, 101343.

Rybnicek, R., & Chung, A. L. (2019). A mixed-method approach to understanding community stakeholder perspectives of satellite remote sensing for conservation. Journal of Environmental Management, 236, 45-55.

Sand, M., & Richard, M. (2016). Communicating environmental risks: Clarifying the severity effect in risk perception. British Journal of Social Psychology, 55(3), 448-464.

Snow, N. (2019). Digital Public Diplomacy: Promoting Peace in the 21st Century. London, UK: Rowman & Littlefield.

Starbird, K., et al. (2014). Rumors, False Flags, and Digital Vigilantes: Misinformation on Twitter after the 2013 Boston Marathon Bombing. iConference 2014 Proceedings.

Stelma, J. (2021). The Digital Diplomat: Understanding the Use of Digital Platforms in Cultural Diplomacy. International Studies Perspectives, 22(1), 25-46.

Wang, Y. (2020). Social Media and Misinformation: A Threat to National Security? Homeland Security Affairs, 16(1), 1-20.

Websites

Council of Europe. (2021). Cybersecurity Education for Diplomats. Retrieved from https://www.coe.int/en/web/cybercrime/cybersecurity-education-for-diplomats

Cornell University Library. (2021). Digital Literacy Resources. Retrieved from https://digitalliteracy.cornell.edu/

Council on Foreign Relations. (2020). Diplomacy in the Digital Age. Retrieved from https://www.cfr.org/report/diplomacy-digital-age

Diplomatic Courier. (2018). Diplomatic Hackathon. Retrieved from https://www.diplomaticourier.com/diplomatic-hackathon

EEAS. (2021). Digital Diplomacy. Retrieved from https://eeas.europa.eu/digital-diplomacy_en

European External Action Service. (2021). Digital Diplomacy. Retrieved from https://eeas.europa.eu/digital-diplomacy_en

Munich Security Conference. (n.d.). Munich Security Conference 2021 Special Edition. Retrieved from https://securityconference.org/en/

UNESCO. (2020). Ensuring Inclusive and Equitable Quality Education and Promoting Lifelong Learning Opportunities for All. Retrieved from https://en.unesco.org/gem-report/report/2020/inclusion#:~:text=In%202018%2C%20over%20160%20countries,universal%20primary%20and%20secondary%20education.

United Nations Department of Economic and Social Affairs. (2020). Digital Technologies and Sustainable Development. Retrieved from https://www.un.org/development/desa/dpad/wp-content/uploads/sites/45/publication/WESS2020_Chapter2.pdf

United Nations. (n.d.). United Nations General Assembly. Retrieved from https://www.un.org/en/ga/

World Economic Forum. (2021). Blockchain in Diplomacy. Retrieved from https://www.weforum.org/agenda/2021/03/why-diplomats-should-embrace-blockchain-and-how-they-can-do-it/

Organization Reports

Ministry of Foreign Affairs of Denmark. (2020). Digital Diplomacy Handbook. Retrieved from https://um.dk/en/foreign-policy/digital-diplomacy/digital-diplomacy-handbook/

Ministry of Foreign Affairs of the Netherlands. (2020). Artificial Intelligence in Diplomacy. Retrieved from https://www.government.nl/topics/artificial-intelligence-ai/documents/reports/2020/05/01/artificial-intelligence-in-diplomacy

United Nations Institute for Training and Research. (2019). Virtual Reality for Diplomatic Training. Retrieved from https://unitar.org/event/full-catalog/virtual-reality-diplomatic-training

Wouters, J., & Defraigne, P. (2020). The Legal Framework of Digital Diplomacy. In J. Wouters, J. Pauwelyn, & T. Ramopoulos (Eds.), The Oxford Handbook of International Organizations (pp. 1-23). Oxford, UK: Oxford University Press.

www.ingramcontent.com/pod-product-compliance
Lightning Source LLC
Chambersburg PA
CBHW051601250726
48653CB00004BA/1266